Gardening for Bumblebees

Dave Goulson

GARDENING
FOR BUMBLEBEES

*A Practical Guide
to Creating a Paradise
for Pollinators*

3 5 7 9 10 8 6 4 2

Square Peg, an imprint of Vintage,
20 Vauxhall Bridge Road,
London SW1V 2SA

Square Peg is part of the Penguin Random House group of companies
whose addresses can be found at global.penguinrandomhouse.com.

Penguin
Random House
UK

First published by Square Peg in 2021

Penguin.co.uk/vintage

A CIP catalogue record for this book is available from the British Library

ISBN 9781529110289

Typeset and designed by Anna Green at Siulen Design

Illustrations on p6 and cover by Maria Stezhko, Ekaterina Stanchenko,
Bonitas and CarlosR, all © Shutterstock.

Printed in China by C&C Offset Printing Co., Ltd.

Penguin Random House is committed to a sustainable future for our
business, our readers and our planet. This book is made from Forest
Stewardship Council® certified paper.

Contents

ACKNOWLEDGEMENTS

Thanks in particular to Pieter Haringsma, who took many of the best photographs of bees, and to Marta Rossi, Steven Falk, and Laurie Jackson, who also provided some lovely pictures. The fuzzier ones are all mine.

Introduction

I have been fascinated by bumblebees since I was only five or six years old, and I have been studying them as a scientist for nearly thirty years. Bumblebees are big, furry and beautiful, their buzzing, lazy flight the perfect soundtrack to a summer's day pottering in the garden or walking in the countryside. There are twenty-six different species to be found in the UK, of about 250 species known world-wide. If you look carefully, it is easy enough to find six or seven species in your garden or in your local park, provided there are a few flowers to attract them. You can see huge queens in the early spring, followed later by their smaller workers, and then males with fluffy yellow faces idling about on flowers in high summer.

Bumblebees are among the most important of our insects, for they are superb pollinators, ensuring that wildflowers set seed and reappear each year, and also that our vegetable and fruit crops give us bountiful harvests. We should therefore be deeply concerned by declines in the populations of our wild bees. Some bumblebees, such as Cullum's bumblebee and the short-haired bumblebee, have gone extinct in Britain. Recently Franklin's bumblebee, a species from North America, went globally extinct. Many species hang on as tiny populations in scattered nature reserves, unable to cope with the stresses of the modern world. We need to look after these endearing creatures, and provide them with refuges where they can feed, breed and thrive.

The good news is that this is easy to do, for it is possible to make any garden into a haven for bumblebees and other wild insects. It doesn't matter how small it is; even a growbag on a balcony can produce copious flowers and attract hungry bees to a nutritious feast. Our gardens and our city parks could all become part of a vast network of pollinator-friendly habitats. Britain has about 22 million gardens, plus about 300,000 allotments, amounting to about half a million hectares of land. In writing this book it is my hope that I will inspire and encourage a few more gardeners and allotment-ers to make their patch more bee-friendly. Perhaps one day all our gardens will be so, and our urban children will grow up able to take for granted the buzzing drone of bumblebees.

Garden produce dependent on insect pollinators:

Crop	Short-tongued bumblebees	Long-tongued bumblebees	Honey bees	Solitary Bees	Others
Almonds	•		•	•	
Apples	•		•	•	flies
Apricots	•		•	•	
Aubergine	•				
Blackberries	•		•	•	flies, beetles, wasps, butterflies
Blueberries	•				
Blackcurrants	•		•	•	
Broad beans		•			
Cherry	•		•	•	
Chili peppers	•				
Courgette	•	•	•		
Cucumber	•	•	•		
Damson	•		•	•	
Gooseberry	•		•	•	
Kiwi fruit	•		•		
Loganberries	•		•	•	
Medlar	•		•	•	
Passion fruit	•		•	•	moths, wasps
Peach	•		•	•	
Pears	•		•	•	
Plum	•		•	•	
Pumpkin	•	•	•	•	
Quince	•		•	•	
Raspberry	•		•	•	
Redcurrant	•		•	•	
Runner beans		•			
Squash	•	•	•	•	
Strawberry	•		•	•	flies
Sweet pepper	•				
Tomato	•				
White currants	•		•	•	

CHAPTER ONE

What is a Pollinator?

All organisms must reproduce, one way or another. If they did not, their species would have long since disappeared. For most animals, finding a member of the opposite sex is relatively easy: we can walk, fly, hop, crawl or run in search of one. Of course, persuading a potential partner to actually mate with us may be much harder. For plants, this process is made much more complicated by the fact that they are, literally, rooted to the ground; they cannot set off in search of a mate.

The act of sexual reproduction requires the transfer of sex cells, known as gametes, from one individual to another. The sex cells in male animals are known as sperm, and they must find and fuse with the egg cell of a female to produce an offspring. In plants, the male sex cells are known as pollen, and they must somehow find their way to a female ovule to produce a seed. Some plants, such as grasses and coniferous trees, cast their pollen onto the wind and hope that chance will blow it to the female parts of another plant. Their pollen tends to be very light, and sometimes has wings or other strange appendages to help it catch the breeze. Nonetheless, wind pollination is a spectacularly inefficient process, and far more than 99 per cent of their pollen goes to waste. As a result, wind-pollinated plants have to produce vast quantities of pollen, and it is these clouds of tiny wind-borne pollen that cause hay fever.

Around 140 million years ago, during the age of the dinosaurs, the blind stumblings of evolution came up with a new solution to this problem. Plants began to harness insects to transport their pollen from plant to plant. By that time insects were probably enormously abundant, and many of them could fly, buzzing about among the forests of conifers, monkey puzzle trees and cycads. Some of them, no doubt, nibbled on the flowers of plants, or on the nutritious pollen, and in moving from plant to plant they accidentally transferred pollen grains. These early flowers would have been tiny and green, as are the flowers of grasses today, for they were not adapted to attract insects. Some plants started producing sugary secretions to encourage more insects to visit, and coloured petals to advertise the reward, and an arms race began between the plant species to attract the most insects. The world burst into colourful bloom.

The earliest of these pollinators were not specialist flower visitors. They were probably opportunistic omnivores, perhaps beetles, and the earliest flowers we know of were the ancestors of today's magnolias. Over time, ever more elaborate blooms evolved, with diverse colours and complex petals. Pollen became larger and stickier, designed to cling to insects rather than float on the breeze. Meanwhile, some of the insects began to specialise in feeding only on pollen and nectar. By about 120 million years ago the first bees had appeared: insects that feed exclusively on pollen and nectar, not just as adults, but also during their immature stages. Bees are essentially wasps that became vegetarian.

Today, about three-quarters of the different types of crops that humans grow around the world benefit from pollination by insects. Some, such as almonds, produce almost nothing without them. About one-third of the food we eat depends upon them. Imagine a world without blueberries, tomatoes, blackberries, raspberries, avocados, strawberries, cucumbers, blackcurrants, pumpkins, chili peppers, coffee and chocolate. Life would hardly be worth living! And those are just a few of the many crops that would be affected if pollinators were to disappear. It would not only be humans that were affected; nearly 90 per cent of all wild plant species also require pollination. Without pollinators, our meadows and hedgerows would have no colourful flowers and, more importantly, ecological systems would collapse. Einstein, it is claimed, once said that 'If the bee disappeared off the face of the Earth, man would only have four years left to live.' There is considerable doubt as to whether he ever really said this, and one might debate whether it is precisely accurate, but it makes the point nicely: bees and other pollinators are profoundly important to our own wellbeing.

CHAPTER TWO

Pollinator Diversity

There is no more quintessential sound of summer than the lazy drone of bumblebees, buzzing from flower to flower among the lavender and catmint of a herbaceous border, or amid the clovers and vetches in an old hay meadow. But listen carefully. The buzz of a bumblebee is deep and low, but there are other noises too: the slightly higher-pitched buzz of honey bees, and the shrill hum of other, smaller insects, all going about their business, moving from flower to flower. If you get down on your hands and knees and look closely, you will soon realise that there are all sorts of different insects visiting the flowers in your garden. The bumblebees tend to be most obvious: they are large, and many have colourful yellow stripes and coloured bottoms – red, white or rusty brown. Honey bees are usually common enough, too – these slim, brownish insects are of course the ones that give us honey, and that are kept in hives around the world.

But this is just the tip of the iceberg: there are also leafcutter bees, sweat bees, mason bees, mining bees, cuckoo bees, carpenter bees and many more – about 270 species in total in the UK. Globally, there are an astonishing 20,000 known species of bee (and no doubt many more yet to be described by science). The large majority are solitary creatures, the female making her own small nest, rather than living in a colony with a queen and workers as do honey bees and bumble-bees. Most people go their whole lives without even noticing these little creatures, yet they live all around us, they pollinate our garden flowers and vegetables, and they ensure that wild flowers set seed.

Bees are the best known of pollinators, and they get the lion's share of the attention, but there are many others. Of the rest, butterflies are perhaps the most familiar, though they aren't particularly important pollinators in Europe. Their mostly nocturnal cousins the moths are both more numerous and a little more important as pollinators; pale, heavily scented flowers such as honeysuckle are often pollinated by them. Then there are the 256 different UK species of hoverflies: fast-moving, beautiful insects, many mimicking bees or wasps with their yellow and black stripes, they tend to visit shallower flowers than bees. On top of them there are the numerous beetles, wasps and flies that pollinate flowers. It has been estimated that there are at least 4,000 species of pollinator just in the UK; no-one has even attempted to work out the likely global total. They are all important: each tends to visit different flowers, to thrive in different places, to come and go in different years. Elsewhere in the world, birds such as hummingbirds, parrots and nectar-eaters have become important pollinators too, and even some types of bat and marsupial mice have got in on the act. Nevertheless, insects remain by far the most important pollinators.

It is humbling to reflect that we know little or nothing about most of the million-or-so insects that have so far been named. New ones are catalogued every day, and there are probably several million species waiting to be discovered. Of those that have been, usually all we have is the name and a reference specimen on a pin in a museum; we have no idea what they do. There must be hundreds of thousands, perhaps millions, of species that are involved in pollination. There have been many scientific studies of honey bees, and quite a few on buff-tailed bumblebees (because they are common and fairly easy to breed in captivity, and so are relatively easy to study). Even in the UK, the most intensively studied country in the world, with a long history of ecological research, we know little or nothing about the natural history of most of our 4,000-or-so pollinators. We often do not know what flowers they prefer, and whether they actually pollinate the flowers they visit. An insect, bird or bat might visit a flower without transferring pollen, perhaps because it is the wrong shape and does not come into contact with the reproductive parts of the plant (in which case it is not a pollinator, though this distinction is often ignored). Of course, even if a particular fly or beetle visits flowers but does not pollinate them, it may perform some other purpose: for example, it might be food for birds or spiders, or help control pests, or recycle dung. As we don't really know what most insects do, it would seem wise to do our best to look after them, since they may turn out to be important. Even if some of them are not, they still deserve their place, I would argue, just as much as we do. Surely we have a moral duty to look after our fellow travellers on planet Earth?

CHAPTER THREE

The Bumblebee Year

It is late October. We have not yet had the first frost here in the south of England, and from my study window I can see the last common carder bumblebees feeding on the Michaelmas daisies. Very soon it will be over for another year.

But it's not long before the bumblebee year starts again. In four months' time, in late February if the sun shows her face, the first bumblebees will emerge from their winter hibernation. They will be starving hungry, for they have been living off their fat reserves for at least six months, often as much as eight. The few flowers around are vitally important: winter heathers, hellebores and crocus are among those in bloom and may be mobbed by ravenous queen bees. The first queens to emerge are usually buff-tailed bumblebees or white-tailed bumblebees, but in March they are joined by all the other common bumblebees: early bumblebees, common carders, red-tails, tree and garden bumblebees. This is the time of year when pussy willows bloom, the first really major source of wild forage for bumble-bees, followed by lungwort and flowering currants.

Provided they can find sufficient food, the queens then search for a nest, flying just above the ground, in a characteristic side-to-side trajectory, scanning for holes. If they find one they crawl inside to investigate, hoping to find a dry, dark, safe cavity, with an old mouse or vole nest inside. I suspect that such holes are often in short supply or are hard to locate, for often on sunny days in early spring there can be dozens of queens quartering the ground, investigating any dark opening but usually emerging disappointed.

If they find what they are looking for, they settle down to nest. Each queen gathers a ball of pollen and lays a batch of eggs in it, covering them in wax. She incubates them much as a bird would, pressing her body against her brood and shivering to generate heat. All being well, the eggs hatch into little white grubs, and she then has to dash out repeatedly to collect more food for them and for herself. It is a precarious time: she must leave her brood unprotected, getting colder by the second, and if there are not enough flowers nearby then her nest is likely to fail. Those queens that succeed are rewarded, about a month after laying their first batch of eggs, with their first adult workers, all daughters. These take over the foraging, and for the rest of her life the queen remains in her nest, laying more eggs and tending to them. Thus it is that around April most of the queens disappear, save for a few stragglers who have failed to find a nest or woken up late, and the smaller workers become common. The nest

Bumblebee nest

grows through spring, accumulating more and more workers. Nests of some species, such as the buff-tailed bumblebee, can grow to have as many as 400 workers, while others, such as the early bumblebee, rarely have more than fifty or sixty.

Eventually the queen decides that it is time to stop producing workers and switch to producing new queens and males. Most bumblebee species do this in July or August, but the early bumblebee and the tree bumblebee switch much earlier, in May or June. The young males and queens fly from the nest and mate, most queens mating just once with a single male. A few days after mating these young queens burrow into the soil to wait, alone in a small chamber in the earth, right round until the following spring. For the males, mating is their only purpose in life – they do no work for the nest – but they often hang around through late summer, long after the young queens are gone, sitting listlessly on flowers sipping nectar.

Eventually the old queen dies, perhaps thirteen months after she was born. The workers too die off one by one, and the old wax and any remaining food stores in the nest are consumed by caterpillars, woodlice, mites and beetles. By October, completing the cycle, the last nests are all but gone, but if all has gone well each nest will have left a legacy of young queens, safe underground, waiting for spring.

There are some bumblebees that, in the last thirty years, have abandoned this annual cycle. Some buff-tailed bumblebee queens have begun emerging from hibernation in the late autumn, feeding on the exotic winter-flowering shrubs we grow in our gardens. If I press my nose to the glass of my study window and squint sideways I can just see a *Mahonia* bush which will come into flower in December, and every year a few buff-tailed bumblebee workers miraculously appear to gather its pollen and nectar. It seems these bees have adapted to the new winter food supply, which historically would have been absent, and are able to cope with chilly winter weather. I have even seen them foraging when there is snow on the ground. I shall have some bee company for the winter months, to tide me over until the bumblebee year buzzes into life once more in early spring.

CHAPTER FOUR

Causes of Pollinator Declines

Given that there are few more important creatures on Earth than pollinators, it is deeply worrying that they are in trouble. The modern world poses many threats to bees and their kin: our countryside has far fewer flowers than it once did, and far fewer quiet places for them to nest. Almost all of our hay meadows and flower-rich chalk downland were ploughed up in the twentieth century, and thousands of miles of hedgerows were dug out. Those hedgerows that remain are awash with fertilisers applied to the neighbouring fields, and so tend to grow only coarse, aggressive plants that thrive in fertile conditions such as nettles, docks and hogweed. Herbicides enable farmers to grow weed-free crops, and where wild flowers do persist in the field margins and hedgerows they are often contaminated with cocktails of insecticides, often including incredibly powerful neurotoxic insecticides called neonicotinoids, which paralyse and kill bees or, even at lower doses, leave them dazed, confused and unable to navigate. New generations of insecticides are continually invented, each supposedly better than the last, but they all kill bees.

On top of this we have accidentally introduced new parasites and diseases from abroad that attack both honey bees and our wild, native bees, and other pollinators too. Viruses such as deformed wing virus spread from honey bee hives to wild pollinators, while an Asian bee disease called *Nosema ceranae* is now causing lethal diarrhoea in our wild bumblebees.

If all of this were not enough, bumblebees prefer cool climates, and do not enjoy the hotter summers and more severe droughts we are already experiencing, which are set to get much worse as climate change really kicks in.

Put these things together, and our poor bees are overheated, weakened by infection and struggling to find food. When they do find something to eat, it is likely to be contaminated with a cocktail of poisons. Small wonder that pollinators are not faring well in our modern world.

It is easy to feel helpless in the face of the many terrible environmental issues that beset our planet, but we can all help to save our bees. They may face a range of threats, but if we can alleviate any of these they will be better able to cope with the rest. Grow some of the flowers described later in this book – ones that are rich in nutritious nectar and pollen – and your bees will be better able to shake off infections. Make sure that this food is pesticide-free by avoiding using pesticides in your garden, and you will dilute the effects of any poisons they may pick up from elsewhere. Provide them with nest sites and with luck you will be rewarded with the sight of their comings and goings as they gather food for their offspring from your garden flowers. This book aims to give you all the knowledge you need to make your garden into a paradise for bumblebees and other pollinators. Together, we can make sure that our bees have a future.

CHAPTER FIVE

Bee Watching

It is well worth taking the time to simply sit down and watch the bees in your garden. Pull up a garden chair by the flower border on a warm day, have a cold drink to hand, and just watch what they are doing. One of the first things you will notice is that there are lots of different types: brown bees, big bees, tiny black ones, ones with yellow and black stripes, others that are black with a red bottom. It always astonishes me that so many people labour under the misapprehension that there is just one species of bee, when a few seconds' observation of a patch of flowers would make it clear that there are many. Of course, you won't just see bees: most flower beds will also attract hoverflies of various types, and also bristly flies, and perhaps some assorted beetles, thrips, wasps, day-flying moths and butterflies.

Take a little time to watch this throng of insects carefully, and you can discover much about their biology, and perhaps find out something brand new. Some of my most interesting discoveries as a scientist originated from just watching bees for the fun of it. In fact, my professional interest in bees sprang from idly watching bumblebees visiting comfrey flowers, nearly thirty years ago. I noticed that the bumblebees often flew close to a flower, but at the last minute would veer away, without ever touching it, as though something was wrong. They might do this several times before finding a flower more to their liking, and landing to drink the nectar or collect the pollen.

I've since found that this is very common behaviour, on all sorts of different flowers – anyone can see it, but seemingly no one had actually *noticed* it. I wondered what they were doing. What was wrong with the flowers they avoided?

It took the best part of five years to unravel exactly what was going on, much of the work being done by my PhD student, Jane Stout. We found that the flowers the bees avoided tended to have little nectar in them, but we also found that the bees weren't able to directly sense nectar levels in flowers. What they were doing was sniffing the petals of the flower for the faint whiff of a previous bee visitor. It turns out that bees accidentally leave behind a smelly footprint when they land on a flower, composed of oily hydrocarbons from their cuticle. Other bees can detect this, and the smell of a recent footprint tells them that the flower is likely to be empty, so they don't bother landing. It saves them perhaps half a second, which may not sound like much, but a bee may visit 10,000 flowers in a day, so it all adds up. This discovery was all brand new to science – yet bees have been doing this right under our noses for as long as we've been growing flowers. I found that very exciting.

Darwin liked to watch bees. Indeed, he seems to have been generally fascinated by almost all of nature, but bumblebees turn up particularly often in his writing. He describes how individual bees tend to visit flowers of the same species over and over again, even when in a patch with lots of flowers all mixed up together. To this day, there are debates as to exactly why they do this. The favoured theory is that bees have to learn how to find the rewards in each type of flower, and that if they keep switching between flower types they would need to keep pausing to recall how to deal with each one, which costs them valuable time. As one entomologist once said, for bees, 'Time is honey.'

Darwin was also the first to describe the peculiar courtship behaviour of bumblebees, getting his children to help him record the 'patrolling' flights of male bumblebees which raced around an established route in his garden in Kent. He was one of the first to notice nectar-robbing, whereby some types of bumblebee such as the buff-tailed will bites holes in the sides of flowers to steal the nectar.

They do this because some flowers attempt to hide their nectar in deep tubes where it is beyond the reach of the short tongue of buff-tails. Darwin saw that honey bees, which have weak mandibles and so are unable to bite through flowers, would nonetheless use the holes made by buff-tails to steal nectar for themselves. Much more recently, my students found that individual bees tend to be either left- or right-'handed' when robbing, almost always biting a hole in the same side of flowers. No-one had noticed this before.

Who knows what you might see if you take the time to look? You don't have to be a scientist to find out new things. Recent years have seen a surge of interest in 'citizen science', in which scientists work together with members of the public to gather data and answer interesting scientific questions. For example, in the Galaxy Zoo project, members of the public helped scientists to classify the shapes of some of the billion or so galaxies visible with powerful telescopes, revealing much about the nature of our universe. Similarly, in Project Discovery, people helped work out how different proteins fold as part of an online game. For the scientists, projects like this offer a way to get far more done than they could possibly achieve on their own; for example, in its first six weeks Project Discovery had 300,000 people do the work it would have taken one person 163 years to do. For the volunteers, these projects can be fun and educational, so everyone benefits.

There are a number of citizen science activities relating to pollinators. In iSpot, people can upload photographs of wildlife and identify photos taken by others, thereby helping to gather information on the distribution of our animals and plants while gaining identification skills themselves. The Bumblebee Conservation Trust runs a similar scheme focused specifically on bumblebees called BeeWatch, and also has a more advanced option known as BeeWalks. In the latter, volunteers are asked to take a monthly walk along the same route, counting and identifying bumblebees. In time, this will enable us to see how numbers of bumblebees are changing over time, and how this varies across the country – all vital information if we are to look after them.

Buzz Club is a small citizen-science club that I help to run, in which we ask our members to assist us in projects to find out how best to encourage pollinators. Among others, we've run nationwide experiments to find out which types of 'bee hotel' are best, how effective 'hoverfly lagoons' are in providing breeding habitat for hoverflies, and whether companion planting boosts pollination of strawberries. All the activities are simple, fun and designed for all ages.

New citizen-science projects appear all the time, so anything I write here may be out of date by the time you read it. A quick internet search will get you up to date on what projects are currently running.

Whether you do it as part of a formal project or just for your own edification, I would urge you to take a little time to watch the bees and other insects in your garden. Who knows what you might discover?

CHAPTER SIX

Common Garden Pollinators

Because there are so many types of insects that pollinate flowers, even just in the UK, learning to identify them is daunting and bewildering. Many are tiny and/or very similar to one another, making them hard to identify even for experts. Below, I provide a quick introduction to some of the bigger and easier-to-identify species you might come across. If you want to go further, thankfully there are some excellent identification guides now available for the UK's bees, butterflies, moths and hoverflies, which provide much more information on each species (see 'Further Reading').

Bumblebees

Being big and colourful, bumblebees tend to be among the most obvious and abundant visitors to garden flowers. It is perhaps surprising, then, especially since there are only twenty-six species in the UK, that bumblebees can be tricky to identify; unhelpfully, some species look very similar to one another. To make matters worse, coat colours vary within species and the fur becomes bleached with age, or sometimes begins to wear thin, so older bees can look quite different from young ones. On top of that, males can look quite different from workers or queens. It is easy to become confused and despondent!

Don't be put off: with a little practice and persistence it is fairly easy to identify most of our common species. If you would like to have a bash at identifying bumblebees, I recommend making life easier for yourself by starting in the early spring, when only the queens are on the wing. They are the big ones, on whom it is easier to spot distinguishing features, and the absence of males or workers at this time of year makes the whole business less confusing. Here I describe the eight most common UK bumblebees, which cover ninety-nine per cent of the bumblebees you might see in your garden or local park.

Buff-tailed bumblebee

Buff-tailed bumblebee, *Bombus terrestris*

By far the commonest bumblebee in almost all the UK and much of Europe, the buff-tailed bumblebee is probably what most people imagine when they hear the word 'bumblebee'. The queens, in particular, usually greatly outnumber queens of other species in early spring, and are the easiest to identify. Buff-tailed bumblebees are black with two golden-yellow stripes and, on the queen, a buff-coloured tail. Unhelpfully, the workers have a more-or-less white tail, which makes them almost impossible to distinguish with certainty from the white-tailed bumblebee (see below). It's not worth getting stressed over – even professionals struggle. The males resemble workers, and so are also quite tricky to identify with certainty.

Buff-tailed bumblebees have a short-tongue and so tend to visit shallow flowers, but they are also enthusiastic nectar-robbers, using their sharp and powerful mandibles to bite holes in the side or back of deep flowers such as comfrey and *Aquilegia* to steal the nectar. Buff-tailed bumblebees usually nest deep underground, following mole, rabbit or rodent burrows to find safe, cosy cavities. Their nests can get large, containing up to 400 workers. Buff-tailed bumblebees are common in almost any habitat with flowers throughout the British Isles, absent only from the far north-west of Scotland.

This species is the basis of a global commercial trade, with millions of nests reared in factories in the Netherlands and Belgium and sold to countries as far away as Japan and Chile, mainly for pollination of glasshouse crops such as tomatoes. Unfortunately, as a result of this trade buff-tailed bumblebees have become an invasive pest in Japan and South America.

White-tailed bumblebee, *Bombus lucorum*

A close relative of the buff-tailed bumblebee, the white-tailed bumblebee is even more widespread, occurring throughout the UK, including the far north-west and Scottish islands where buff-tails are absent. However, this species tends to be much less abundant, particularly in the south. The queens of the two species are fairly easy to distinguish, the white-tailed bumblebee living up to her name and having a snow-white tail. The two yellow bands are also slightly brighter than in the buff-tailed, and often described as lemon yellow, though the difference is subtle. Separating the workers is where the problem lies, for the only difference between them and the workers of the buff-tailed bumblebee (which, remember, have whitish tails) is the colour of the yellow bands. Males of the white-tailed bumblebee resemble the workers, but they have a fluffy yellow face, and often the yellow bands are much thicker, so their overall appearance can be very yellow.

The ecology of white-tailed bumblebees is similar to that of buff-tails. They too have short tongues and are incorrigible nectar-robbers, so one way or another they visit a broad range of flowers. Their nests are usually underground, but they also commonly seem to nest under the wooden floor of garden sheds.

Early bumblebee, *Bombus pratorum*

Early bumblebee queens have two yellow stripes with a rusty red tail, a unique combination of colours in springtime. They are notably smaller than queens of superficially similar species such as the buff-tail. The workers are similar in appearance to the queen, although sometimes the second yellow band is very faint or absent. Early bumblebees are one of our smallest bumblebees, and some workers can be tiny. Males have fluffy yellow faces and thicker yellow bands, making them very handsome little bees.

Early bumblebees have short tongues and so tend to visit shallow flowers. Queens are often seen on pussy willow and flowering currants, while the workers and males are particularly fond of raspberries, cotoneaster and geraniums. Early bumblebees have blunt jaws and cannot bite holes to rob nectar, but in my garden they routinely use holes bitten by other bees to rob nectar from comfrey. Their name derives from the fact that early bumblebee colonies never grow very large, and finish their annual cycle in May and June, with

White-tailed bumblebee

Early bumblebee

the first males appearing as early as the end of April in a warm year. There sometimes seems to be a very small second generation, but on the whole this species is not seen past early July. They nest opportunistically in all sorts of places, either in cavities just below or above the ground – for example under stones in a rockery – or sometimes well above the ground in tit boxes or old bird's nests. Early bumblebees are extremely placid, not attacking even if their nest is disturbed.

Red-tailed bumblebee, *Bombus lapidarius*

Queens of the red-tailed bumblebee are very distinctive, being large and entirely glossy black except for their bright red tail. The workers are identically coloured, while the males have a yellow face, a thick yellow band behind the head, and a smaller yellow band at the back of the thorax (the section of an insect behind the head). With their red tail the males are very attractive bees, superficially similar to male early bumblebees but on the wing much later, usually from late July onwards.

Red-tailed bumblebee queens tend to emerge a little later than the former species, usually in April. This species has a short tongue and is particularly fond of legumes such as bird's-foot trefoil, and is also one of the commonest bumblebees visiting oilseed rape crops. Interestingly, red-tails seem to have a strong preference for yellow flowers. Red-tailed bumblebees are generally the most numerous bumblebee species in farmland, and especially on chalk downland, where the males can be hugely abundant in August, often sitting in groups on knapweed and thistle flowers. Red-tailed bumblebees are most common in the south, and scarce in Cumbria and much of Scotland. They nest both above and below ground, often under large stones or in gaps in walls.

Garden bumblebee, *Bombus hortorum*

Garden bumblebees are superficially similar to white-tailed bumble-bees, but have three yellow stripes (rather than two) along with the white tail. Workers and males all have this same pattern, the males sometimes having a bit of yellow on their head too. The head of the garden bumblebee is elongated, almost horse-shaped, unlike that of any other common bumblebee, and a consequence of this is that they have a very long tongue, up to 15 mm, which they use to extract nectar hidden in the depths of tubular flowers. As a result, they tend to visit quite different flowers to most other bumblebees, giving a strong clue to their identity. The queens love white dead-nettle in early spring, while workers visit foxgloves, honeysuckle, red clover and snapdragon. If you want to see a garden bumblebee then pretty much all you have to do is watch a foxglove when in flower and, so long as the day is warm, within a few minutes you can almost guarantee one will turn up.

Garden bumblebees are found throughout the UK, although they are rarely abundant. They emerge from hibernation in April and build nests on or just above the ground, sometimes occupying tit boxes. The nests never grow very large.

Red-tailed bumblebee

Garden bumblebee

Tree bumblebee, *Bombus hypnorum*

The tree bumblebee is perhaps the easiest bumblebee species to identify, sporting a unique and distinctive colour pattern. In the queen and workers the thorax is a rich, foxy brown, and the abdomen is black with a white tail. Males are identical or very similar, the only difference being that sometimes the brown extends onto the front of the abdomen.

This species was not found in the UK until by chance I caught the first one at the edge of the New Forest in 2001. Since then it has spread rapidly, reaching southern Scotland, and has become a very common garden species. It is named after its habit of nesting in holes in trees, but it readily adopts tit boxes and also commonly enters the eaves of houses to nest under the loft insulation. Males of the tree bumblebee hang about in excited crowds outside nests that are producing virgin queens, sometimes causing considerable concern to homeowners, who frequently call for assistance in dealing with the 'swarm'. In reality the males, which have no sting, are completely harmless, and since the nest is releasing young queens it will soon disappear of its own accord.

The tree bumblebee has a short tongue and so tends to prefer shallow flowers, particular favourites being pussy willow, chives, cotoneaster, bistort, geranium and *Ceanothus*. This species has a short colony cycle similar to the early bumblebee's, so tree bumblebees are generally done for the year by the end of June.

Common carder bumblebee, *Bombus pascuorum*

The common carder bumblebee is rather drab compared to other species, being entirely brown with a sprinkling of black hairs (in queens, workers and males). Nonetheless, I find this species particularly endearing. It has two very scarce cousins, the brown-banded carder and the moss carder, that are similarly coloured, but these are highly unlikely to turn up in a garden, so you can be pretty sure any all-brown bumblebee you see is a common carder.

Common carders have medium-length tongues, preferring flowers which have hidden their nectar in tubes where short-tongued species struggle to reach it. Among their favourites are clovers, dead-nettles, woundworts and catmint. They typically nest just above the ground in tussocky grasses, under leaf-litter and in bramble thickets. Common carders seem to adopt a different strategy to other bumblebee species in that their nests grow slowly, but carry on growing until late summer and even into autumn. As a result, this species tends to be the last bumblebee on the wing each autumn (excluding the winter-active buff-tailed bumblebee queens that emerge in November).

Southern cuckoo bumblebee, *Bombus vestalis*

There are six species of cuckoo bumblebee in the UK, each of them parasitic on a particular host bumblebee species. Cuckoo bumblebees are aptly named, for like their namesake bird they commandeer the nests of others.

Female cuckoo bumblebees (there are no queens or workers) emerge from hibernation a little later than their hosts, and search for a host nest. Once they have located one, they enter and attempt to take over, killing the resident queen or bullying her into submission. Female cuckoos are, therefore, particularly large and powerful insects. They also differ from their hosts in lacking a pollen basket on their hind legs, as they do not bother collecting food for their brood.

Once she has taken charge of a nest, the female cuckoo eats any eggs laid by the old queen and lays her own, while the workers of her host become her slaves, continuing to collect food and look after the new brood laid by the invader. The cuckoo's brood comprises more of the powerful females and much smaller males, both of which leave their natal nest and mate much as other bumblebees do. The young mated queens then hibernate until the following spring.

In England and Wales the southern cuckoo is usually by far the most common cuckoo, presumably because its host, the buff-tailed bumblebee, is usually our most abundant species. Cuckoos tend to roughly resemble their hosts in colour. The southern cuckoo female is black with a thick yellow band behind the head, and a white tail which has a yellow fringe at the forward margin. The males are similar, but with an extra yellow band at the front of the abdomen. However, identifying cuckoo bee species with certainty is tricky, and requires reference to a specialist guide (see Further Reading). Males of the southern cuckoo are seen far more often than the females, and can be very abundant on bramble flowers in July.

Southern cuckoo bumblebee

Bumblebee identification charts

The UK currently has 24 species of bumblebee, all illustrated over the charts on the next three pages (extinct species are not shown). The most common species are on the first two charts, and these are the ones most likely to be seen in gardens. Six of the 24 species are cuckoo bumblebees that parasitise other species – they are shown on the third chart. Some of these can be common, especially the southern cuckoo. Sadly, bumblebees are in decline – three species not shown here are extinct and several more are threatened.

Queens and males (♂) are shown on the diagrams. Unless otherwise stated, workers are just smaller versions of the queens.

Common bumblebees

Buff-tailed bumblebee, *Bombus terrestris*.

Very common.

Worker or ♂

Queen

Red-tailed bumblebee, *Bombus lapidarius*.

Common.

♂

Queen

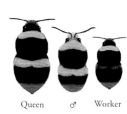

Early bumblebee, *Bombus pratorum*.

Common. Yellow band on abdomen of worker often absent.

Queen ♂ Worker

Garden bumblebee, *Bombus hortorum*.

Common. Very long tongue and face.

Queen

White-tailed bumblebee, *Bombus lucorum* complex.

Only queens of these three species can be identified, by looking at the side of the thorax – see right.

Queen ♂

White-tailed bumblebee, *Bombus lucorum*. Common.

Cryptic bumblebee, *Bombus cryptarum*. Common.

Northern white-tailed bumblebee, *Bombus magnus*. Common in N & W. Note that these characters are not 100% reliable.

Common carder bee, *Bombus pascuorum*.

Very common everywhere. Usually black hairs on sides of abdomen.

Queen

Heath bumblebee, *Bombus jonellus*.

A small bee, widespread on heaths, moors and sometimes in gardens. Short face compared to garden bumblebee.

Queen

Rare bumblebees

Broken-belted bumblebee, *Bombus soroeensis.*

Declining northerly species. Similar to buff or white-tailed, but smaller. Yellow band on abdomen extends further forwards at sides, and is sometimes broken in the middle.

Queen

Queen   Queen   Queen

Ruderal bumblebee, *Bombus ruderatus.*

Rare southern species. Very long face and tongue. Queens very large. Variable colour patterns.

Hard to distinguish from garden bumblebee; note shape of yellow band at rear of thorax.

Queen

Brown-banded carder bee, *Bombus humilis.*

Rare southern species. Note brown band.

Queen

Moss carder bee, *Bombus muscorum.*

Very rare except on some Scottish Isles.

Queen

Shrill carder bee, *Bombus sylvarum.*

Very rare southern species. Noticeably high-pitched buzz.

Queen

Bilberry or blaeberry bumblebee, *Bombus monticola.*

Rare mountain species.

Queen

Red-shanked carder bee, *Bombus ruderarius.*

Rare southern species. Note red hairs on hind leg.

Tree bumblebee, *Bombus hypnorum.*

Recent immigrant from France spreading north.

Queen

Queen

Great yellow bumblebee, *Bombus distinguendus.*

Very rare Scottish species.

Cuckoo bumblebees

Southern cuckoo bee, *Bombus vestalis.*

Common in south. Attacks mainly buff-tailed bumblebees.

♀

♀　♂

Forest cuckoo bee, *Bombus sylvestris.*

Widespread. Attacks mainly early bumblebees.

Red-tailed cuckoo bee, *Bombus rupestris.*

Southern species. Attacks mainly red-tailed bumblebees.

Females have very dark wings compared to red-tailed bumblebees.

♂　♀

Barbut's cuckoo bee, *Bombus barbutellus.*

Widespread. Attacks mainly garden bumblebees.

♀

♀　♂　♂

Field cuckoo bee, *Bombus campestris.*

Widespread. Attacks mainly common carder bees. 2 male forms occur.

♀　♂

Gypsy cuckoo bee, *Bombus bohemicus.*

Widespread. Attacks mainly white-tailed bumblebees.

Bumblebee or Cuckoo, male or female?

Some tips: **Look at the hind legs.** Female bumblebees have a shiny black pollen basket surrounded by long hairs. Males have less-pronounced 'baskets', longer antennae, and no sting. Cuckoos have **no pollen baskets** and darker wings.

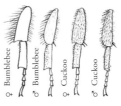

♀ Bumblebee　♂ Bumblebee　♀ Cuckoo　♂ Cuckoo

Solitary bees

Most people are surprised to learn that there are about 270 species of bee in the UK. We tend to notice the bumblebees, because they are big and often colourful, and we have all seen honey bees and bee hives, but many of us have never noticed the majority of our bee species, for they tend to be small. Unlike honey bees and bumblebees, most of them lead solitary lives. They have no queen or communal nest. Each female mates, and then constructs her own nest, which may be a burrow in the ground, a hole in a dead tree, a hollow plant stem or even an empty snail shell. Sometimes several females will nest near to one another in nest 'aggregations', but they don't collaborate in rearing their young. Many solitary bees have just one generation per year, meaning that the adults are only on the wing for a short period. If you would like to learn more about these bees, I heartily recommend Steven Falk and Richard Lewington's book *Field Guide to the Bees of Great Britain and Ireland*. I will whet your appetite by introducing just a few of the more distinctive and common solitary bees, all of them species you might well attract into your garden.

Ashy mining bee, *Andrena cineraria*

A fairly common and widespread species, ashy mining bees are a little larger than a honey bee, clothed in grey hairs and with a shiny black abdomen. They have just one generation each year, and are on the wing from late March to June. Like other mining bees, they nest in the ground, preferring bare earth or short turf into which they burrow. Nests can often be found in large aggregations on south-facing slopes. Ashy mining bees have a wide diet, but seem to favour flowering shrubs such as willow, hawthorn, blackthorn and apple. They can be important pollinators of oilseed rape fields.

Hairy-footed flower bee, *Anthophora plumipes*

These are delightful bees, one of my favourites. They are amongst the largest of solitary bees, easily mistaken for a smallish bumblebee, but their darting flight is quite distinctive, fast and interspersed with hovering. They have a single flight season, appearing alongside the first queen bumblebees in early spring, sometimes as early as February, and are highly attracted to lungwort, and then a little later in the year to dead-nettles and ground ivy. Females are entirely black apart from a prominent orange pollen-brush on their hind legs, while the males are largely pale brown. The mid-leg of males has a fringe of very long hairs near the foot, which he uses to stroke the face and cover the eyes of the female during mating. The hairy-footed flower bee is fairly common in southern England, but has been recorded as far north as Ayrshire. It constructs pitcher-shaped nests from compacted soil, usually on coastal cliffs, clay banks or in the soft mortar of an old brick wall. Nests of several females may often be clustered together.

Ivy bee, *Colletes hederae*

This pretty bee was described as new to science in 1993, but is now known to be widespread in much of Europe. Quite simply, it seems no-one had noticed it before. It was first recorded in the UK in 2001, coincidentally the same year tree bumblebees were first seen. Since then it has spread as far as the north Midlands and South Wales, and become very common in the south, often occurring in large numbers in gardens. It is always the last bee of the year to appear, emerging at the end of August and remaining on the wing into November. Its late emergence is timed to coincide with the flowering of ivy, which is the preferred pollen and nectar source, though ivy bees do visit a broad range of other autumn flowers too, including garden asters. This species is relatively easy to recognise, having a thorax covered in golden hairs and a neatly striped gold and black abdomen.

Ivy bees burrow into the ground to nest, often using lawns and flower borders, and some nest aggregations in the south have become

Clockwise from top left:
Ashy mining bee
Hairy-footed flower bee
Ivy bee
Leafcutter bee

very large, filling entire gardens. Bee activity around these aggregations can be considerable, the females coming and going with pollen and males hanging around trying to mate with them. Newly emerged virgin females can find themselves mobbed by hundreds of males, which form a ball around them. All these bustling bees can alarm homeowners, who in extreme cases call for pest control, but there is no need to be alarmed. The females are capable of stinging, but they almost never do, and the sting is much less painful than that of a honey bee. It's quite possible to continue gardening in the midst of an aggregation without being stung. I have ivy bees foraging on the hedge in front of my house every autumn. As yet I have found no nests in my garden, but I would love them to move in.

Leafcutter bee, *Megachile willughbiella*

This is the most common of several species of similar bees, called leafcutters after their habit of snipping neat semi-circles of leaf with which to line their nests. They are of similar size to a honey bee, and clothed in greyish brown hairs. Leafcutters carry pollen among dense hairs on the underside of their abdomen, rather than on their legs as honey bees or bumblebees do. They have a distinctive way of repeatedly lifting their abdomen high in the air when feeding on flowers, seemingly showing off their pollen-covered tummy. Males are similar, without the hairy underbelly but with white, hairy front feet, which make them look as if they are wearing clean white gloves. This species has one generation per year, flying from late May to August. It is generally abundant across most of England, but scarce in Wales and Scotland. Leafcutters tend to have broad diets, particularly liking pea-family plants such as bird's-foot trefoil, and also thistles, knapweed and brambles. They nest in holes, and are frequent users of bee hotels if the earlier-emerging red mason bees have not occupied them all first. Their nests are easily distinguished: mason bee nests are plugged with mud, while leafcutters block their tunnels with bundles of snipped leaves. In my garden their favourite leaves for this are lilac and rose.

Nomad bees, *Nomada marshamella*

There are seventy-three different species of cuckoo bee in the UK, six of them cuckoo bumblebees (which attack bumblebee nests), the remainder cuckoos of our many solitary bee species. Cuckoos specialise in attacking just one or two closely related host species. Typically, they locate a nest and sneak in to lay their own eggs when the owner is away foraging, the cuckoo offspring then consuming both the host's offspring and their food store. Many cuckoos are relatively scarce – they have to be rarer than their hosts – and are often small, so are easily overlooked. In my experience the cuckoos most likely to turn up in your garden are nomad bees, a large group of very wasp-like yellow and black or yellow-, orange-and-black-striped, almost hairless bees. They do not visit as many flowers as ordinary bees since they don't have to gather food for their offspring, but nonetheless they are often seen feeding on daisy-family plants and umbellifers. Most nomad bees attack mining bees, and the presence of female nomads skulking around is usually a good sign that nests of their host are nearby.

Red mason bee, *Osmia bicornis*

One of the commonest of our solitary bees, the red mason bee is the main resident of most 'bee hotels'. They are quite furry little bees, a touch smaller than a honey bee. Females have a black head, brown thorax and reddish/orange abdomen, while the males are similar but with a whitish face. They have one generation per year, the adults emerging in March and active until early July.

This species seems to be particularly associated with gardens and urban areas, being quite hard to find in the countryside. Red mason bees visit the flowers of a broad range of plants, but particularly like spring-flowering trees such as sallows, plums, apples and pears. They are said to be much more effective pollinators of fruit trees than honey bees, and a small commercial trade has developed in rearing this species for fruit pollination. Red mason bees

Top to bottom:
(l) Nomad bee
(r) Red mason bee
Tawny mining bee
Wool carder bee

nest in naturally occurring holes and crevices, such as beetle holes in dead wood, cracks in the structure of garden sheds, holes in the soft mortar of old walls or hollow plant stems. The females collect damp soil to line the nest tunnel, to separate each brood cell and to seal the hole once they have finished. They have horns on their face specifically for manipulating mud. In my garden a stream of them go to the hollow where a tree was blown over in a storm, ripping its roots out of the ground and leaving a deep, damp hole that, thankfully, I never thought to fill in.

Tawny mining bee, *Andrena fulva*

The females of this species are perhaps the easiest solitary bee to identify, being about the same size as a honey bee but clothed in a dense orange/red fur, with a black head and legs. The males, smaller and less furry than the females and resembling several other mining bees, are trickier to identify. Tawny mining bees are quite common, often occurring in gardens and parks, and even in densely urban areas. Like many other mining bees, they have a single generation per year, the adults being on the wing from March to June, and visit a wide variety of spring flowers including hawthorn, blackthorn, fruit trees and willow. In my garden they are often the most frequent pollinator of my gooseberries, blackcurrants and redcurrants. The nest burrows are usually in aggregations in bare ground or lawns, the females creating neat cones of spoil material that can upset very tidy-minded gardeners.

Wool carder bee, *Anthidium manicatum*

These are splendid, sturdy bees, about the length of a honey bee but much chunkier, mostly blackish with bright yellow spots along the sides of the abdomen. They have one generation per year, and are on the wing from May to August. Wool carders are fairly frequent in much of England and Wales, but are more common in the south, and regularly turn up in gardens. In general, male bees (and for that matter male insects) tend to be smaller than the females. The females need to be big to produce lots of eggs, while the males need to be agile to chase females. Wool carders, however, are an exception: the males are bigger, and armed with spikes on their abdomen. They are fiercely aggressive, defending patches of flowers by hovering over them and attacking any intruding bees with head butts or by using their spiked abdomen to crush their foe in mid-air, sometimes killing them. On the continent I have seen them drive off carpenter bees that must have been five times their size. Female wool carders that wish to visit the flower patch have to mate with the resident male.

Wool carders are strongly associated with woundworts, particularly lamb's ear, which they visit not just for the flowers but, in the case of females, to collect the woolly white hairs that clothe the leaves. They'll also collect hairs from great mullein. They nest in ready-made holes, often in man-made objects, although oddly they rarely use bee hotels. I sometimes have them nesting in downward-facing holes in my garden picnic table. The hairs are used to line their nests and to separate each grub.

Honey bee, *Apis mellifera*

While there are several species of honey bee found in Asia, in Europe we have only one. The honey bee is of course the bee kept by apiarists, and from which we obtain honey. It is a very unusual species, forming huge colonies which might have as many as 50,000 workers as well as the queen. It is the only social bee in Europe in which colonies survive the winter, and this is why honey bees make lots of honey – to keep them going through the winter months. In spring, healthy colonies left unmanaged will naturally split, sending out a swarm containing a queen and several thousand workers who will attempt to start a new colony. Beekeepers generally do their best to prevent this, as they don't want to lose the bees. In the wild, honey bees nest in hollow trees or in caves. Honey bees now struggle to survive in the wild in much of Europe, although there are occasional colonies resulting from swarms escaping from domestic hives, and these often occupy cavities in buildings.

If hives are kept near to your garden you will often find honey bees are the commonest bees you see. They are fairly easy to recognise, being much more slender than a bumblebee, with much sparser hair, usually of a pale tan colour.

There is plentiful evidence that honey bees can compete with our wild pollinators, taking much of the available pollen and nectar, particularly when large numbers of hives are kept together. Honey bee hives can also spread diseases to wild insects. I don't want to discourage anyone from keeping honey bees, for it is a fascinating and enjoyable hobby, and I love to eat honey myself, but do bear these issues in mind. If you do have honey bee hives, try and make sure you provide lots of flowers so there is plenty of food to go around. As an approximate rule of thumb, one honey bee colony will use all the nectar and pollen in half a hectare of flower-rich habitat.

Hoverflies, *Syrphidae*

There are 256 species of hoverfly in the UK, slightly fewer than the number of bees, and many of them among the more colourful and attractive insects you might spot in the garden. A number of them are excellent mimics of wasps or bees, a strategy they use to put off potential predators, who are fooled into thinking they have a sting. It is not uncommon to see images of hoverflies mistakenly used in the media to illustrate articles about bees or wasps, so clearly their disguise is effective, to some humans at least. Hoverflies can be distinguished from bees and wasps by their larger eyes, tiny antennae and possession of only one pair of wings (bees and wasps have two).

Batman hoverfly, *Myathropa florea*

This yellow and black hoverfly has a distinctive black mark across the thorax closely resembling the stylised bat symbol used by Batman. This is a common species throughout the UK, flying from May to October. The adults seem to particularly like white flowers, including many umbellifers, hawthorn and bramble. The larvae are aquatic, living in rot-holes in trees, sap runs where sap is leaking from a damaged tree trunk, or small puddles. They have a long, hair-like breathing tube attached to their rear end which they use like a snorkel, and which gives the larvae their common name of rat-tailed maggot (also used for larvae of the drone fly and tiger hoverfly – see below). The larvae probably feed on the bacteria that thrive on rotting leaves and other organic material.

Bumblebee hoverfly, *Volucella bombylans*

A magnificent hoverfly, one of the largest, and pulling off a superficially convincing impression of a bumblebee. Two colour forms exist: one that is black with a red tail, closely resembling a red-tailed bumblebee, and one that is black with yellow stripes and a white tail, resembling a white-tailed bumblebee. They even copy the bumblebee habit of raising a middle leg when they are disturbed and too cold to fly away. Eggs are laid in bumblebee or wasp nests and, if the female hoverfly is killed while entering the nest, she automatically lays all of her remaining eggs. The ugly, spine-covered maggots scavenge in the bee or wasp nest and generally don't do any harm, so far as anyone knows; by removing waste they may even benefit their hosts.

The bumblebee hoverfly is quite common across the UK, having two generations per year and being on the wing from May until September. It feeds on a wide variety of flowers, including umbellifers, bramble, knapweed and scabious.

Batman hoverfly

Bumblebee hoverfly (both colour forms)

Common snout-hoverfly, *Rhingia campestris*

The prominent, beak-like extension of their face, combined with an orange abdomen with a black line down the sides, makes this one of our most easily recognised hoverflies. This species has elongate mouthparts, which enables it to feed on deep flowers such as bugle, dead-nettles and red campion – flowers most hoverflies avoid – though I often also see them feeding on shallow flowers like apple blossom. The larvae of this species breed in cow dung, and perhaps in the dung of other animals. The common snout-hoverfly is, as the name suggests, an abundant species, found in gardens in both rural and urban areas from April to October. Keep an eye out also for the less common sister species *Rhingia rostrata* (distinguished by the absence of the black line along the sides of the abdomen). The life cycle of this latter species is entirely unknown – no larva has ever been seen, though it seems likely that they live in some kind of dung, should you wish to look for them.

Drone fly, *Eristalis tenax*

One of the commonest hoverflies throughout the UK and throughout the world, the drone fly is very often mistaken for a honey bee, being of similar size and colour. Its large eyes give it a closer resemblance to male honey bees, known as drones, than to the more commonly seen worker honey bees – hence the name. Drone flies can be seen throughout the year, since the females hibernate as adults in nooks and crevices and will pop out on warmer days in the depths of winter. Drone flies feed on a great variety of shallow flowers, particularly umbellifers, and are often found in huge numbers on ivy flowers and Michaelmas daisies in autumn. In the spring and summer, males sometimes defend territories, and have a characteristic behaviour in which they hover, stationary, in the air for prolonged periods. Like those of the batman hoverfly, the larvae are aquatic, and breathe through a siphon attached to their rear end. They live in small puddles containing rotting organic matter, or in wet dung and

Common snout-hoverfly   *Drone fly*

Hornet hoverfly

sewage, and sometimes occupy artificial 'hoverfly lagoons'. Note that there are several similar species within this genus.

Hornet hoverfly, *Volucella zonaria*

The largest hoverfly in the UK, this eye-catching species is a good mimic of our native hornet, with a yellow-and-black-striped abdomen, brown thorax and yellow face. This species was considered a rare migrant to the UK from southern Europe until the

1940s, when it became established here. It has now become quite common in the south, and regularly turns up in gardens and parks, even in densely urban areas, from May through to October; it is frequently seen in London parks and gardens. As with the bumblebee hoverfly, the maggots are scavengers that live in the nests of social insects, in this case the nests of the common wasp (*Vespula vulgaris*). Interestingly, there is no evidence of them living within the nests of hornets. The adults are very often seen feeding on buddleia, and will also visit a range of other flowers, including hemp agrimony, devil's bit scabious, brambles and roses.

Marmalade hoverfly, *Episyrphis balteatus*

A slender, delicate hoverfly, superficially resembling a wasp with its yellow and black stripes. The marmalade hoverfly is easily recognised by two slender black bands on the abdomen, which each resemble a moustache. This is the most common and widespread hoverfly in the UK, and has been recorded in every month of the year, although of course it is more common in summer. In some years the UK population of this species is boosted by huge numbers of migrants from the continent. Marmalade hoverflies will feed on a wide range of shallow flowers, including ragwort, dandelion, hawkbits and cow parsley. They seem to be most commonly attracted to yellow flowers. Their maggot-like, greenish, semi-transparent larvae are not beautiful to behold, but are very important biocontrol agents in both gardens and farm crops, being specialist predators of aphids. Planting, for example, single-flowered French marigolds (*Tagetes)* or lovage to attract the adults is therefore a great, environmentally friendly way to protect your veggie crops from harm.

Tiger hoverfly, *Helophilus pendulus*

This species is also known as 'the footballer', both names deriving from the distinctive longitudinal black and yellow stripes on the thorax.

Marmalade hoverfly

Tiger hoverfly

This is a handsome and common fly found throughout the UK from April to November. The tiger hoverfly has catholic tastes when it comes to flowers, visiting forget-me-nots, daisy-family plants such as thistles, hawkbits, dandelion and asters, and also devil's bit scabious and ivy. This is one of the most common species to occupy artificial hoverfly lagoons, with adult males often setting up territories and defending lagoons in the hope of mating with any females that wish to lay eggs in them. The aquatic larvae have shorter breathing tubes than the drone fly. There are five similar species in this genus.

Other flies

There are over 7,000 species of fly in the UK, and no doubt many hundreds could be found in any UK garden if one had the time and patience to look, but identifying most is a specialist task. Flies are most certainly not most people's favourite insect, but they are important nonetheless. A great many visit and pollinate flowers; others do vital jobs such as recycling dung and carrion, and are food for many larger organisms such as swallows, flycatchers, frogs and bats.

Dark-edged bee fly, *Bombylius major*

This is my absolute favourite fly, a lovable, furry, flying powder-puff of brown hair that hovers like a hummingbird, using its long proboscis to probe flowers for nectar. They can be confused with bumblebees, although the long rigid proboscis and darting, hovering flight are clear giveaways. Bee flies are on the wing in spring, from March to June, and are commonly seen in gardens, sunning themselves on the ground or flying from flower to flower. Their proboscis enables them to drink from deep flowers such as lungwort, primroses, grape hyacinth and red campion, though they are not particularly fussy.

Female bee flies hover close to the nests of mining bees, and flick their abdomen to fire eggs into the entrance tunnel. Like cuckoo bees, their developing grub consumes the host's larvae and their food. Sometimes the eggs are placed on flowers, and then the young bee fly larvae latches onto visiting bees and hitchhikes back to their nest. There are several related species in this genus, but all except the dark-edged bee fly are scarce and unlikely to be seen in gardens.

Wasps

There are in the region of 7,000 species of wasp in the UK, from tiny parasitoid wasps just a couple of millimetres long to queen hornets which may be nearly 4 cm in length. They all have two pairs of wings, fairly obvious antennae, and usually a narrow waist. A great many different types of wasp may be seen drinking nectar or eating pollen on flowers, although we have little idea how many of them are important pollinators. As with the flies, identifying most of them is beyond the scope of the amateur (and indeed most professional entomologists). The majority of wasps are solitary insects, but there are a handful of species that live in large social colonies with a queen and workers, which include the typical yellow-and-black-striped insects that most people imagine when they hear the word wasp.

Common wasp, *Vespula vulgaris*

There are four similar species within this genus, but this is the most abundant, common throughout England, Wales and the warmer parts of Scotland. The life cycle is similar to that of bumblebees, with colonies being founded single-handedly by queens in March, and fizzling out in autumn after producing new queens and males. Unlike bumblebees, these wasps use wood pulp rather than wax to build their nest, which is usually located in a dry, dark cavity, often in loft spaces or little-used garden sheds, or in a hole in the ground such as a rabbit burrow. These social wasps are sometimes bothersome at picnics, and will readily sting if you disturb their nest, but nonetheless we should try to appreciate them, because they can be important pollinators, and also because they are major predators of caterpillars and aphids, both pests of vegetable crops. These wasps can be amongst the most abundant insect species visiting ivy flowers in autumn. Earlier in the year, I find, they are fond of fennel flowers, along with other umbellifers.

Beetles

There are more than 4,000 species of beetle in the UK, and many hundreds of these feed on flowers. A handful of the more common and distinctive ones are described below. As a group, beetles are quite distinctive: their forewings are heavily modified into wing cases, usually shiny and hard, underneath which the hind wings are neatly folded when not in use. This gives them a characteristic shape, often rounded and with no wings visible.

Rose chafer, *Cetonia aurata*

Rose chafers are jewel-like, large and stocky metallic-green beetles streaked with white. The underside is an equally beautiful golden/copper colour. As in most other iridescent, metallic-coloured insects, the colour is created through the diffraction of light by striations on the surface of the cuticle, rather than by pigment. This is not a common species in the UK, but turns up regularly in gardens in scattered sites across England and South Wales. The adult beetles love the pollen of roses, brambles and hogweed, and are on the wing in late spring and summer. Their flight is distinctively clumsy and noisy. The fat white grubs live in rotting tree stumps, compost and leaf mould, eating the slowly decaying organic matter. Unusually for an insect, the life cycle often takes two years to complete.

Soldier beetle, *Rhagonycha fulva*

Soldier beetles are easily recognised, elongate rust-coloured beetles with black tips to their wing cases. They are generally by far the most common beetles visiting flowers in my garden. They are on the wing from late spring to early autumn, and spend much of their summer locked together in mating pairs, while simultaneously grazing on the pollen of umbellifers and daisy-family plants. They particularly

Top to bottom:
Rose chafer
Soldier beetle
(l) Swollen-thighed flower beetle
(r) Wasp beetle

like lovage, cow parsley, hogweed and creeping thistle. In addition to feeding on flowers, soldier beetles prey on small insects such as aphids, and provide valuable pest control in the vegetable patch. The larvae are also predatory, eating slugs and snails, and so also provide a valuable service to the gardener. The larvae prefer to live amongst dense, tussocky grass, so having a meadow area is a good way to ensure plenty of them.

Swollen-thighed flower beetle, *Oedemera nobilis*

These are beautiful, elongate, metallic-green beetles, which spend much time grazing on flowers and can be found across the southern half of Britain from April to August. They seem to particularly like hogweed, brambles, ragwort and ox-eye daisy. Their name derives from the swollen hind legs of the male beetle, though what purpose these serve is unclear. The larvae feed within the dried stems of thistles and probably other pithy-stemmed plants.

Wasp beetle, *Clytus arietis*

As the name suggests, these handsome insects pull off more than a passing resemblance to a wasp, having bright yellow stripes against a black background. As with hoverflies, the mimicry is all bluff, as they have no sting or other defence. Wasp beetles are moderately common throughout England and Wales, and are most often seen browsing on the flowers of umbellifers such as wild carrot, lovage, angelica or parsnips left to flower. Their grubs burrow in dead wood, so leaving an old log pile or unfelled dead trees can help encourage this species.

Small copper

Butterflies

Butterflies and their cousins the moths all belong to an insect order known as the Lepidoptera, meaning scaly wings. This may not sound appealing, but in fact the beautiful colours of their wings are created by the coloured scales in which their wings are clothed, and which come off in a smear on your fingers if you touch them.

For many, butterflies are the most desirable of insects to attract to the garden. As a child, I recall the buddleia in our garden attracting dozens of peacocks, small tortoiseshells, red admirals and white butterflies. Sadly, there is no doubt that the numbers of garden butterflies are far lower than they once were, but if you plant the right flowers you can still expect to see some beauties. Plant a buddleia and all of the species above are likely to turn up occasionally, plus, perhaps, commas and painted ladies. Marjoram is another magnet for butterflies: if you live anywhere near large, open spaces or have a big garden then marjoram may attract gatekeepers and meadow browns, common blue butterflies, and even marbled whites and ringlets if you are very lucky. Ragwort is also great, popular with skipper butterflies and small coppers, while thistles and knapweed attract a broad range of butterflies.

Perhaps the most valuable thing a gardener can do is provide suitable flowers in autumn and early spring for those species that spend the winter as hibernating adults. Ivy and ice plants are important autumn resources that are particularly attractive to red admirals and small tortoiseshells stocking up for their winter sleep. In early spring, dandelions, pussy willow and bluebells are great to welcome them out of hibernation with a sugary drink.

You may also be tempted to splash out on one of the many 'butterfly hotels' or 'butterfly boxes' which can be purchased these days, either online or in garden centres, and are intended to provide suitable hibernation places for butterflies. Some are very attractive to the human eye, but in my experience butterflies show not the slightest interest in them.

With bees, providing them with suitable flowers and a bee hotel to nest in caters for almost all their needs, but for butterflies a different strategy is required. They do not need a hotel and, although they enjoy flowers, most scientists think butterfly populations are usually probably not limited by availability of nectar. They need to sip from a flower now and again to top up their energy but, unlike bees, do not need to gather large quantities of nectar for their offspring, and have no interest in pollen. The key resource they often lack is food plants for their caterpillars. Some suggestions of butterfly food plants easily accommodated in a wildlife garden are given in the chapter 'Providing breeding sites for other pollinators'.

Below are the butterfly species most likely to turn up in a suburban garden:

Hesperiidae

Commonly known as the 'skippers', this is an endearing family of small, slightly moth-like butterflies which have a fast, darting flight and often perch in a characteristic position with their wings half open. In the UK, most skipper species are associated with meadows, and the caterpillars of the majority of species feed upon grasses.

Large skipper   *Small skipper*

Large skipper, *Ochlodes sylvanus*

Handsome, orange-brown insects, these are distinguished from the related small skipper by their larger size and chequering of the wings with patches of darker brown. The males can be pugnacious, perching on a prominent leaf in a sunny spot, and dashing out aggressively at any passing insect. Large skippers are on the wing in July and August, spending nearly eleven months of the year as a slow-growing, inconspicuous, brownish caterpillar. The caterpillars make a shelter for themselves by using silk to draw blades of grass into a protective tube, and hence are not easy to find. Their preferred food plant is cock's foot (*Dactylis glomerata*), and the butterfly is commonly found wherever this plant is left uncut, in woodland rides and clearings, field margins, overgrown churchyards and rough grassland. You will need a meadow area in your garden if you are to have much chance of attracting this species. Large skippers are widespread in England and Wales, but only occur in the far south of Scotland.

Small skipper, *Thymelicus sylvestris*

Like its larger cousin, the small skipper is a butterfly of high summer, being on the wing from June to August, with just one generation per year. The charming golden-brown adults are commonly seen drinking nectar on a range of flowers, including meadow vetchling, thistles and ragwort. Like the large skipper, the small skipper spends most of its life as a caterpillar hiding in tubes of grass, in this case particularly favouring Yorkshire fog (*Holcus lanatus*), which fortunately is also a very common grass species. The small skipper is found in rough grasslands, field edges, road verges and sunny woodland rides – almost anywhere grasses are allowed to grow long. If you'd like to attract them to breed in your garden, a small patch of long grass in a sunny spot may well do the job. Small skippers are common throughout England and Wales, but are almost entirely absent from Scotland.

Lycaenidae

Commonly known as 'the blues', this is a large family containing small, delicate and sometimes exquisitely beautiful butterflies, many of which are blue, but some of which are brown, and others metallic copper. The caterpillars of many 'blue' butterflies have complicated mutualistic relationships with ants, which defend them in return for protein-rich secretions that the caterpillars exude.

Common blue, *Polyommatus icarus*

Gorgeous little butterflies, with the uppersides of the males' wings sky-blue fringed with black and white, while those of the females are either blueish or chocolate brown with orange spots. The undersides of both sexes are pale brown, decorated with an intricate pattern of white, black and orange spots. Sadly, the 'common' blue is not quite as common as it once was, but it still regularly turns up in gardens in the urban fringe and rural areas. In the countryside it is primarily a species of flower-rich meadows, but it also frequents brownfield sites, overgrown churchyards, road and rail cuttings and sand dunes. This species squeezes in two or three broods per year, with peaks of abundance in June, August and late September. The larvae feed on a range of legumes, including clovers, but their favourite food is bird's-foot trefoil, a very easy plant to grow, and one you can naturalise in a meadow area (planting amongst the grasses and flowers) or cultivate in a herbaceous flower bed.

Holly blue, *Celastrina argiolus*

Most of our native blue butterflies are associated with grasslands, but the holly blue is an exception, being found fluttering around holly bushes and established ivy on walls and trees. The uppersides of the wings are a lovely, warm sky blue, but are hard to get a good look at as this species rarely sits with its wings open. The underside, which is all one can normally see, is a very pale bluish grey with small black spots.

It is by far the earliest blue butterfly on the wing each year, so if you see a smallish blue butterfly in April or early May it is certain to be this species. These spring adults lay their eggs on holly, with the caterpillars eating the buds, berries and leaves, and a second generation of adults appears in August, which lay their eggs on the buds of ivy flowers. In warm years there can be a partial third brood on the wing in October, particularly in the south of England. Holly blues are still fairly common in gardens, parks and churchyards throughout the southern half of Britain, though numbers cycle through regular peaks and troughs over a four-to-six-year cycle, driven by the specialist parasitoid wasp *Listrodomus nycthemerus*, which attacks only the holly blue and periodically builds up in numbers. You can encourage the butterfly simply by allowing ivy to grow and flower, and avoiding pruning outside the winter months if it must be done at all. If you are really keen, plant a holly tree too.

Common blue   *Holly blue*

Small copper, *Lycaena phlaeas*

A feisty and beautiful little butterfly, the small copper is unmistake-able, with its metallic copper wings dotted with brown spots. Males are highly territorial, perching on a prominent stem and attacking any other butterfly that dares to encroach on its personal space. The small copper is widespread throughout the UK, except in mountain-ous areas, although rarely common. It has three generations per year, so that adults are almost continuously on the wing from late April to October, tending to become more common as the year progresses. The caterpillars feed on common sorrel and sheep's sorrel, which is worth growing as it also makes a spicy addition to salads. This species tends to prefer warm, well-drained places, and turns up on rough grassland, brownfield sites, heathland, rough grassland, sand dunes and quarries. I usually have a few in the meadow area of my garden, where the adults love to nectar on ragwort flowers.

Nymphalinae

Many of our most familiar and colourful butterflies belong to this cosmopolitan family. They tend to be powerful fliers; many hibernate as adults, and in the UK most of them feed upon nettles. Oddly, they generally use only four of their six legs, the front pair being held folded under the head.

Comma, *Polygonia c-album*

One of my favourite butterflies, the comma has elaborately sculpted wings that, when it is resting, make it look for all the world like a curled, dead leaf, adorned with a small, white, comma-shaped mark. Commas hibernate as adults, appearing on the wing in the first warm days of March. Eggs are laid mainly on nettles, although historically they were laid mainly on hops, and this species was once considered something of a pest in hop gardens. The odd-looking, spiny larvae are dark brown or orange, with a splash of white that makes them resemble a bird dropping. The comma declined to the point of near extinction in the UK in the nineteenth century, but recovered strongly from the 1930s onwards, starting in the south of England and moving northwards. It is now widespread throughout England, Wales and up to central Scotland, though never abundant. The adults like rotting fruit such as plums, and I have found that they seem to particularly favour nectaring on leek flowers.

Painted lady, *Vanessa cardui*

I can still remember my excitement when I saw my first painted lady as a teenager. It was quite battered, and I imagined the adventures it must have had, for these butterflies migrate to Britain from north Africa every spring. In some years they can become very common by late summer, breeding up on patches of thistles (the caterpillar's main food plant). The caterpillars live hidden within tents of leaves held together with silk, but they are messy creatures, and their droppings accumulated among the silk webbing make the tents easy to spot. Freshly emerged painted ladies are heart-stoppingly pretty, their rich orange wings decorated with a distinctive pattern of black and white. Along with many other butterflies, the adults particularly enjoy buddleia flowers, also enjoying thistles, knapweeds and bramble. They are on the wing from April, when the first keen migrants reach our shores, right through to October, when presumably they drift southwards once more.

Peacock, *Aglais io*

Perhaps the most easily recognised and familiar of UK butterflies, the peacock remains common across Britain. The characteristic blue eye spots that give the butterfly its name evolved to frighten predators. Peacocks hibernate as adults, often entering garden sheds to do so, and, when perched in a corner with their wings closed, resemble a dead leaf. If disturbed by a potential predator like a mouse they flick open their wings to reveal the large eyes, at the same time making a rasping noise by rubbing their wings together. The hope is that the mouse is startled into retreat. It is common for peacocks and their relatives small tortoiseshells to enter houses to hibernate, but modern central heating means that most houses are far too warm and these butterflies will die. If the weather isn't too bad, put them outside. Otherwise, relocate them to a cool shed or other sheltered spot, but make sure it is easy for them to escape when they wake up in spring. The peacock has one generation per year, the gregarious velvet-black and spiny larvae spinning protective webs among nettles, their preferred food, in June and July.

Top to bottom:

Comma

Painted lady

(l) Peacock caterpillars

(r) Peacock

Red admiral

Small tortoiseshell

Red admiral, *Vanessa atalanta*

A very distinctive and handsome species that can be seen throughout the UK. When I was young, it was believed that this species could not survive the winter in the UK, with migrants arriving from continental Europe and north Africa each year in spring. However, regular sightings of adults nectaring in very late autumn, and being spotted again on warm days in winter, suggest that at least some are hardy enough to make it through winter in the south of England. One was discovered alive and well sleeping in a rabbit burrow in February, and others have been seen exiting from rabbit burrows in late winter, so perhaps this is a popular hibernation spot for them. The caterpillar's food plant is nettle but, unlike its relatives the peacock and small tortoiseshell, the caterpillars of the red admiral are solitary creatures, constructing themselves a little tent of nettle leaves sewn together with silk. The adults feed on over-ripe fruit such as blackberries, and are particularly partial to ivy flowers in autumn.

Small tortoiseshell, *Aglais urticae*

When I was young, these were the most common butterflies on the garden buddleia, but they are now much less abundant, although still widespread. The UK's Butterfly Monitoring Scheme shows that between 1976 and 2012 their numbers fell by 76 per cent. Small tortoiseshells have two generations per year and hibernate as adults, so providing nectar-rich flowers like ice plants in late summer helps keep them going through their long sleep. Like those of their relative the peacock, the caterpillars of the small tortoiseshell live among webbing on patches of nettles, but they are easily distinguished by their brownish colour, striped with creamy yellow. As with the peacock, the females lay eggs on young nettle growth, so if you have a large patch of nettles try cutting some of it back hard in early June. This will provide a flush of new growth by the end of the month, which is roughly when the summer brood are looking to lay.

Pieridae

Commonly known as 'the white family', butterflies in this family are usually primarily white or yellow. The *Pieridae* contains some of our commonest butterflies, and the caterpillars of most of them feed on cabbage-family plants. The family includes the only two UK butterfly species that can be regarded as significant pests.

Brimstone, *Gonepteryx rhamni*

The first sight of the flashing yellow wings of a male brimstone each year is a welcome sign that spring is near. These glorious butterflies have just one generation per year, the adults living for about nine months from August to May, and hibernating among foliage. They exhibit what scientists call 'sexual dimorphism', the males being a rich yellow colour on the upperside of their wings while the females are a pale greenish-cream. Both sexes are wonderful mimics of leaves when sitting still with their wings closed, as they do during their long hibernation. Early naturalists called this species the 'butter-coloured fly', and it is claimed that this is the origin of the general term 'butterfly'. If you live in the south or midlands of England or Wales there is a good chance you will see brimstones passing through your garden, and if you grow their larval food plant, buckthorn or alder buckthorn (both shrubs or small trees), there is an excellent chance they will lay eggs, though you will need an eagle eye to spot the very well camouflaged green larvae and pupae.

Green-veined white, *Pieris napi*

One of our most widespread butterflies, and on the wing in two overlapping generations from April through to September, the green-veined white is common in gardens and parks throughout the UK. In the countryside it is also found in woodland rides, scrubland, along hedgerows and, more rarely, in open meadows. Predominantly white on top with black markings, this species is broadly similar to both the small and large white butterflies, but is easily distinguished by the rather beautiful greenish streaks on the undersides of the wings. The green-veined white lays its eggs on a range of wild brassicas (cabbage family), including cuckoo flower, charlock and hedge mustard, but luckily not on cultivated brassicas. It spends the winter as a pupa, attached to a plant stem by a delicate girdle of silk.

Large white, *Pieris brassicae*

The large and small white butterflies are often collectively known as the 'cabbage whites', but they are quite distinct species, both of which happen to be partial to eating our cultivated cabbage crops. The large white is a powerful flyer, with the resident UK population often topped up by migrants flying over from continental Europe. Aside from size, the two species differ in the shape of the black mark on the upperside of the wing tip, which in the large white continues a long way down the wing margin. The caterpillars are much easier to tell apart, for those of the large white are mustard-yellow dotted with black, and live gregariously in large clusters, while those of the small white are green, solitary creatures, much harder to spot. Both species can be kept away from garden cabbages with netting, or for small patches of cabbages it is easy enough to search regularly for the yellow eggs or clusters of tiny holes created by the young larvae, and squash them. You will often be assisted in keeping them under control by the tiny wasp *Cotesia glomerata*, which injects up to fifty eggs into each caterpillar. The unfortunate caterpillar is then consumed from the inside while still alive, the wasp grubs eventually bursting out of their host to spin a cluster of bright yellow cocoons. These wasps do not have it all their own way, for they themselves are parasitised by an even tinier wasp, *Lysibia nana,* so that the caterpillar, *Cotesia* and *Lysibia* are like Russian dolls, one inside the other.

Orange tip, *Anthocharis cardamines*

A lovely spring butterfly, the orange tip spends the winter as a pupa, and is on the wing from April to June with just one generation per year. Male orange tips are unmistakeable, their orange wing tips flashing as they fly, but the females lack this and are superficially similar to a green-veined white. They can be distinguished by the mottling of the underside, which is much more heavily green.

The orange tip lays its eggs on a very similar range of food plants to those favoured by the green-veined white, including cuckoo flower and garlic mustard. These plants are widespread in damper places, including along hedgerows and woodland edges, and this is typically where you most often see the butterflies. The caterpillars prefer to eat the developing seed pods of their host plants, and are relatively easy to find on the senescing flower heads of cuckoo flower. If you have suitable food plants you may well get orange tips breeding in your garden, but beware of too much winter tidying and cutting, because it is very easy to destroy the overwintering pupae, which tend to be attached to a plant stem.

Small white, *Pieris rapae*

Along with its cousin the large white, small whites are a significant pest for our garden cabbages, although they will also eat a range of wild brassicas such as garlic mustard and hedge mustard (see under 'Large white' for tips on telling them apart and controlling them). There are two generations per year, with adults on the wing mainly in May and June and again in August. Small whites are found almost everywhere apart from the Highlands of Scotland, and are most commonly seen hunting around for their food plants in our allotments and gardens.

Top to bottom:
(l) Brimstone
(r) Green-veined white
(l) Large white
(r) Orange tip
Small white

Satyrinae

Meadow brown   *Gatekeeper*

Commonly known as 'the brown butterflies' for the obvious reason that the majority of species are predominantly brown, this family comprises some of our most common and familiar butterflies, like the meadow brown and gatekeeper. However, few of the brown family are likely to regularly breed in gardens, unless you have room for a significant area of meadow. The caterpillars of almost all members of this family feed upon various types of grasses, tend to be well camouflaged in greens and browns, and are nocturnal, so are rarely noticed.

Speckled wood   *Ringlet*

Speckled wood, *Pararge aegeria*

Brownish butterflies with creamy-orange spots, speckled woods are primarily woodland and woodland-edge butterflies that are quite at home in mature gardens and parks, so long as there are some trees and patches of long grass. The speckled wood seems to be one of our more adaptable species: it is the only British butterfly that can over-winter in two life stages, either the caterpillar or the pupa, and it has a flexible number of generations, either two or three depending on location and weather. The adults can be seen from April to October more or less continuously. The males often defend sunny spots in woodland, driving off any other males that might try to move into their territory in aerial battles that spiral upwards. These males can remain in residence for days on end. They rarely visit flowers for nectar, so I wonder how they fuel all their activity. The females are said to lay their eggs on various coarse grasses, but in my garden they show a strong preference for false brome grass, *Brachypodium sylvaticum*.

Ringlet, *Aphantopus hyperantus*

From a distance, ringlets appear to be rather dull brown butterflies, but close up they are a lovely velvety chocolate brown, adorned with clusters of cream-coloured rings. This is a species haunting damp grassland and woodland edges, and I always find a few of them in overgrown corners of my garden, often feeding upon bramble flowers. In common with most of the brown family, ringlets have just one generation per year, with adults flying in July and August. They spend the bulk of the year as caterpillars, slowly munching on grasses such as cock's foot (*Dactylis glomerata*) and false brome grass (*B. sylvaticum*), so they will only breed in your garden if you have some patches of uncut, long grass.

Moths

Moths are often seen as the creepy, dowdy, nocturnal cousins of butterflies, prone to bashing themselves to dusty pieces against lights at night. The 1991 film, *The Silence of the Lambs*, about a serial killer who breeds moths as a hobby, probably didn't help. To further mar their reputation, a couple of species have the audacity to live in our wardrobes, where they chew holes in our woollen clothes. Yet the low regard with which moths are held is undeserved, for many moths are beautiful. True, quite a few are mainly shades of brown, grey and rust, but they have wonderful camouflaged patterns, resembling drying leaves, lichens, dead twigs or bird droppings. Some, such as the burnet and cinnabar moths, are superbly colourful, putting some butterflies, such as the drably coloured meadow brown, to shame. While there are 70 species of butterflies in the UK, there are nearly 2,500 species of moths. If you were to place a moth trap (which uses ultraviolet light to attract moths to a lobster-pot-style trap) in almost any garden in the UK on a warm summer night, you would catch dozens of species, perhaps hundreds. In two nights of trapping in my garden in Sussex a keen moth enthusiast caught 169 different species of moth, from minuscule 'micro-moths' no more than 1 cm long to huge hawkmoths.

Unless you use a moth trap you will never see most types of moth, for the majority are nocturnal, and carefully hide themselves away from predatory birds during the day. A few do fly in the day, and these include some of our most colourful species, like the afore-mentioned cinnabar and burnet moths. It is not coincidence that these colourful species fly in the day: they are poisonous, and use their bright colours to advertise this, so have no need to camouflage themselves and hide away during the hours of daylight.

If you wish to encourage moths in your garden, grow pale flowers that release their scent in the evening, such as honeysuckle, jasmine, white campion, evening primrose and *Nicotiana*. Buddleia is also good, while knapweed will attract day-flying moths like burnets. Lavender and valerian are favoured by the day-flying hummingbird hawkmoth. As with butterflies, it is probably more important to provide food plants rather than nectar for moths, but since there are so many moth species almost any native plants you might grow are likely to be food for some of them. Further details are given in the chapter 'Providing breeding sites for other pollinators'.

A selection of moths that might turn up in your garden and which fly during the day (and are hence the ones you're likely to notice) is given below.

Cinnabar, *Tyria jacobaeae*

Named after the scarlet-coloured mineral cinnabar, a form of mercury sulphide, these unmistakeable scarlet and black moths are commonly found anywhere where the foodplant ragwort grows. The adult moths sit about on flowers, often nectaring on ragwort, and flutter away rather feebly when disturbed, looking as though they might die at any moment. They are on the wing from May to August. Ragwort is a weedy plant of overgrazed meadows, waste ground, railway banks and brownfield sites, and inspection of ragwort plants from June onwards will usually reveal the yellow-and-black-striped caterpillars, initially feeding in groups but then splitting up and living alone as they get bigger. The bright colours of both caterpillars and adult moths are a warning to potential predators such as hungry birds that the insects have stored up the toxic alkaloids that make the ragwort poisonous.

Hummingbird hawkmoth, *Macroglossum stellatarum*

My heart skips a beat every time I see one of these marvellous insects. They do look superficially like hummingbirds, for they are large-bodied moths that fly extremely fast, pausing to hover in front of flowers to drink the nectar. They have large eyes and a very long tongue, more or less the length of their body, which when feeding they hold outstretched in front of them. Their preferred flowers, which include red valerian, lavender, honeysuckle and buddleia, hide their nectar in deep tubes. The eggs are laid on lady's bedstraw, wild madder and hedge bedstraw, and if you are lucky you may find the caterpillars from June to October. These moths are migrants, flooding northwards from the Mediterranean and in a good year getting as far as Shetland. It is thought a few adults manage to hibernate in the south of England in warmer winters.

Mint moth, *Pyrausta aurata*

This small but handsome chocolate-brown moth with golden spots has become moderately common in gardens, although in the wild it is mostly associated with chalk grassland. As the name suggests, its caterpillars eat mint, or related plants such as marjoram, sage, thyme and catmint. You might suppose, then, that they pose a threat to your herb garden, but I've never seen them become numerous enough to cause real harm. The greenish-brown caterpillars hide away by making a tent for themselves from leaves held together with silk. The adult moths themselves often sit around rather conspicuously on mint, and are on the wing in two broods, in May and June, and then again from July to September.

Silver Y moth, *Autographa gamma*

This moth is usually seen as no more than a grey blur, fluttering in a frenzied way from flower to flower. If one ever sits still long enough you might be able to see that is has delicately patterned grey wings with a neat cream letter Y on each forewing. The silver Y moth is a migrant, in most years arriving in large numbers from the Mediterranean from mid-spring onwards. This species must be remarkably tough, for some manage to fly as far as Iceland. Once they arrive here, they breed rapidly, packing in three or four generations before the first frosts kill them off or drive them south. The green, camouflaged caterpillars will eat a wide variety of herbaceous plants, including peas, cabbages and beets, so they are often regarded as a pest, though I find there are rarely enough of them to worry about.

Six-spot burnet, *Zygaena filipendulae*

Gloriously colourful and rather lazy, chubby and slow-flying moths, six-spot burnets can be found throughout the British Isles, often sitting drinking nectar from flowers of knapweed, scabious or thistle.

As with the cinnabar moth, the bright colours are a warning that this moth is poisonous, in this case containing cyanide that it sequesters as a caterpillar from the food plant bird's-foot trefoil. Six-spot burnets are on the wing in high summer, from June to August, and can be very abundant in preferred habitats like flower-rich chalk downland, but they also often turn up in other habitats such as sunny woodland rides, sand dunes, road verges and gardens. The fat yellow and black caterpillars are easy to spot on the foodplant in late spring, as are the papery yellow cocoons which are spun along a tall grass stem. Female burnet moths are often mated within seconds of emerging, while their wings are still unfurling, and the mated couples often hang from the female's empty cocoon.

Top to bottom:
Mint moth
Silver Y moth
Six-spot burnet

CHAPTER SEVEN

The Best Garden Plants for Pollinators

Many familiar garden flowers and wild flowers are excellent sources of nectar and pollen for pollinators. There is a popular misconception that a wildlife garden has to be untidy, overgrown and full of nettles and brambles. This is rubbish (although I must admit that brambles are an absolute favourite with many insects). Bumblebees, butterflies and other wildlife don't care two hoots whether your garden is tidy or not, so long as it provides them with food and shelter. It is perfectly possible to have a garden that is both beautiful and a haven for wildlife. However, many of the garden flowers widely sold in garden centres provide little or nothing for wildlife, so successful wildlife gardening is largely about knowing which are the right kinds of flowers.

If you wish to have happy bees, many of the gaudy bedding plants that are commonly sold outside garden centres, DIY stores and supermarkets are best avoided. For example, *Pelargonium*, *Begonia*, busy lizzies, pansies, petunias, lobelias and the like are all pretty hopeless for pollinators. Over many decades these plants have been subjected to extreme artificial selection by plant breeders aiming to produce larger, more spectacular blooms in a huge variety of colours, or longer flowering periods. Nothing wrong with that, but in the process the flowers have often lost the vital nectar that attracts bees, or the shape of the flower has become so deformed that insects can

no longer reach the nectar or pollen. In extreme cases the flowers are sterile hybrids and produce no pollen at all. Similarly, double varieties are mutants in which some or all of the anthers (the male flower parts that produce pollen) are expressed as extra petals; these can make it impossible for insects to get into the flower, and if they do struggle inside they will be disappointed to find no pollen. The classic 'hybrid tea' rose – the type you might give on Valentine's Day – is a familiar example, but if you browse the plants in your local garden centre you will spot dozens more: there are double holly-hocks, carnations, camellias, *Aquilegia*, *Dahlia* and peonies to name a few. These bundles of petals may look pretty to us, but to a bee they are useless.

For these reasons, single varieties of old-fashioned cottage-garden flowers such as lavender, sage, *Aquilegia* and lupins are generally far better. They are often very similar to the wild flowers from which they originated, and so have not lost their natural link with their pollinators. They also tend to be pretty robust and easy to grow, and the majority are perennials, so you don't have to plant them every year. Most grow well in a traditional herbaceous border, while if you have only a small space there are plenty of pollinator-friendly plants that will grow well in pots on a patio, in a growbag, or even in a window box. Many are useful culinary herbs too: for example, chives, marjoram, sage and rosemary are all loved by bees.

Of course, wild flowers have not been the subject of intensive breeding for traits that appeal to humans, and many of them are very attractive to insects. Wild flowers have become scarce in the countryside through the loss of our hedgerows, hay meadows and chalk grassland, and also because of widespread herbicide use and contamination of the landscape with fertilisers. If you make space in your garden for native wild flowers, you gain the dual benefit of helping conserve both the flowers themselves and the host of creatures they support, including bees.

Some of our rarer pollinator species tend not to visit exotic garden flowers, instead preferring native British wild flowers. Many of these native wild flowers are extraordinarily beautiful, and deserving of a place in the garden regardless of their attractiveness to insects. We often forget that many conventional garden flowers such as foxgloves are native wild flowers, and that all garden flowers have been developed from wild flowers from somewhere in the world.

As with traditional cottage-garden flowers, wild flowers are usually easy to grow, being generally hardy and much more resistant to slugs, mildew and the like than more exotic garden flowers. For example, viper's bugloss (*Echium vulgare*) makes a magnificent plant for a herbaceous border, with spikes of vivid blue flowers up to 2 metres (6 feet) tall that attract a cloud of bees in high summer.

Bee species differ in the length of their tongues, and as a result prefer different flowers. The longest-tongued bee species in the UK, the garden bumblebee (*Bombus hortorum*), has a tongue of about 15 mm, and it loves to drink nectar from deep flowers such as honeysuckle and foxglove. In contrast, short-tongued species such as the early bumblebee, which has a tongue of about 7 mm, have to sip from shallow flowers such as geranium and cotoneaster. A few species, particularly the buff-tailed bumblebee, are short-tongued but practise nectar robbery: they have sharp jaws and bite through the back or side of deep flowers to access the nectar. In my garden almost every comfrey and *Aquilegia* flower ends up punctured with robbing holes. Other short-tongued bees such as the early bumblebee and honey bees, species that are unable to bite holes themselves, often learn to use the holes created by buff-tails so that they too can access nectar illicitly.

The list on the following pages includes what I think are the very best flowers for pollinators, both native wild flowers and cottage-garden plants. So far as possible the selection is based on scientific studies, or at the very least on first-hand experience of seeing large numbers of pollinators visiting the plant. Most of them I have grown myself, and I can verify that, in my garden at least, they are magnets for pollinators. However, there is much we don't know about which are the best varieties. While there have been some side-by-side comparisons of the attractiveness to pollinators of different varieties of lavender and aster, for example, for many common garden plants such as *Campanula* or *Penstemon* there has been no attempt to quantify which species or varieties are best. There is plenty of scope for keen wildlife gardeners to do their own trials.

The list below is far from definitive. Exclusion from it should most definitely not be taken as an indication that something isn't worth growing, for there are undoubtedly many other great plants for pollinators I have yet to discover.

I have grouped the flowers according to plant family, since it is useful to know which tend to be the best plant families for insects. This might help you discover other flowers I have overlooked, but does come at the price of including some rather dauntingly long Latin names.

Plant any one of the flowers below and I guarantee you will attract insects. Grow a few of them, and you will be well on your way to laying out your very own pollinator banquet. The * star ratings indicate my opinion as to the relative attractiveness of these plants to insects, from * = good to ***** = superb. For each plant species I provide some basic tips on how best to propagate them. Further details on these methods can be found in the chapter 'Propagation Techniques'.

Asparagus family, *Asparagaceae*

An obscure plant family containing hyacinths, bluebells and, of course, asparagus. The latter does not need pollinating to produce its edible shoots, but the small yellow flowers are popular with bumblebees.

Bluebell*, *Hyacinthoides non-scripta*

A familiar native perennial plant, famed for the blue carpets of flowers it produces in some of our ancient woodlands in spring. Bluebells are not visited by many insects because their flowers are too deep for most to reach the nectar, and hence even a woodland full of bluebell flowers might have just a few bumblebees buzzing about. Those bees one might see are almost invariably queens of the longer-tongued species such as the garden bumblebee (*B. hortorum*), and for these, bluebells are probably an important source of food. Bluebells are of course perfect plants for growing in a shaded area, particularly under deciduous trees. Avoid buying the Spanish bluebell, which has often been sold in garden centres and which hybridises with our native species. Bluebells can be grown from seed, or multiplied by splitting clumps of bulbs in summer or autumn when the leaves have died back.

Grape hyacinth****, *Muscari armeniacum*

Grape hyacinth is a perennial from southern Europe which is surprisingly hardy in the UK. It is a small plant up to about 20 cm tall, bearing clusters of violet-blue, egg-shaped flowers in spring. Grape hyacinth is an undemanding plant, great for edging a border, sprinkling in a rockery and growing under shrubs such as roses. As well as being attractive to bumblebee queens, grape hyacinths are favoured by two of my favourite spring insects, hairy-footed flower bees (*A. plumipes*) and bee flies (*Bombylius* species). Propagation is easiest via splitting crowded clusters of bulbs once the foliage has died down.

Asphodel family, *Asphodelaceae*

Relatives of the asparagus family, asphodels include the widely cultivated medicinal plant *Aloe vera*, but are otherwise a little-known group of plants.

Red-hot poker***, *Kniphofia*

Strangely, *Kniphofia* were enormously popular garden plants before the Second World War, but fell out of fashion despite being magnificent perennial plants with splendid, architectural, strap-like foliage and dramatic red or orange flower spikes up to about 1.2 m tall. *Kniphofia* originate from southern Africa, and their flowers are intended to attract sunbirds to pollinate them – red is a colour birds find attractive and is often seen in bird-pollinated flowers. The tubular flowers drip nectar and, in the absence of birds, insect pollinators such as honey bees and bumblebees gorge themselves, yet *Kniphofia* feature on very few lists of good plants for bees. *Kniphofia* prefer a sunny position and need good drainage – a sandy soil with added humus is ideal. They can be grown from seed, or propagated by slicing off 'offsets' in early spring; side shoots emerge at ground level on the sides of the main stem.

Clockwise from top left:

Grape hyacinth

Red-hot poker

Borage

Echium pininana

Campanula

Bellflower family, *Campanulaceae*

This family includes several attractive native wild flowers, such as harebells and bellflowers. Analysis of the pollen on old bumblebee specimens suggests that *Campanula* used to be a very important source of pollen for them in the wild, but sadly these flowers now tend to be rare in the countryside.

*Campanula****, bellflower

There are many species and varieties of *Campanula*, and in my experience they are all attractive to bees. They are also rather elegant perennial plants, producing a mass of bell-shaped, pendent, blue or mauve flowers in late spring or summer. Some are great ground cover, growing low and dense and smothering the ground with flowers, while others have tall, nodding, flowering stems up to 1 m. One of my favourites is our native clustered bellflower (*Campanula glomerata*), a lovely plant found on chalk grasslands and dunes. It prefers a well-draining, neutral or alkaline soil, in sun or partial shade. I find that *Campanula* are easy to grow from seed or by splitting clumps.

Borage family, *Boraginaceae*

The borage family, comprising a small number of rather bristly perennial and annual herbs, includes some of the very best plants for bumblebees, such as lungwort, comfrey, borage and viper's bugloss. No bee garden should be without them. Aside from those listed below, others of value to pollinators include forget-me-nots, alkanet and hound's tongue.

Borage****, *Borago officinalis*

Borage is a very easily grown annual herb that drips with nectar and flowers for months on end. It readily self-seeds each year so long as there is a bit of soil disturbance, so one packet of seed should keep you going for a long time. Borage is a native of southern Europe, so it prefers a sunny site, but it will tolerate partial shade. In good conditions it can grow up to 1 m, providing a profusion of vivid blue flowers from early summer until the first frost. Borage is particularly loved by honey bees, and is also popular with short-tongued bumble-bees. The flowers are edible, and make a novel and colourful addition to salads.

Comfrey*****, *Symphytum officinale*, 'Bocking 14'

Comfrey is a very hardy perennial, great for the back of a herbaceous border or a forgotten corner where it will look after itself. In theory it prefers moist locations, but in my experience it doesn't care too much. Comfrey has a very long flowering period, with a peak in late May and June, but then smaller numbers of flowers right through to October. It is a great plant for bees, visited by both long- and short-tongued species, the latter often robbing from holes bitten in the tops of the flowers. Comfrey can be chopped down regularly and used to make excellent potassium-rich compost, or steeped in water to produce a foul-smelling but highly nutritive liquid compost for tomatoes. It sprouts back up vigorously after being cut back, and has a renewed flush of flowering. Comfrey can grow 1.5 m tall or more, and will smother smaller plants nearby. It propagates incredibly easily from root cuttings, and because of this is rather difficult to get rid of should you ever wish to, for even a tiny fragment of root left behind will soon form another plant.

There are other, smaller species of comfrey that are also worth growing, including the cream-flowered Iberian comfrey (*S. ibericum*),

Comfrey

Early bumblebee on comfrey

Iberian comfrey

Caucasian comfrey

Lungwort

Honeywort

which is low-growing and great for providing ground cover in shady areas, and also the attractive blue-flowered Caucasian comfrey (*S. caucasicum*).

Lungwort****, *Pulmonaria officinalis,* 'Blue ensign' or 'Trevi Fountain'

A great nectar resource for hungry queen bumblebees in very early spring, it may also, if you are lucky, attract the wonderful hairy-footed flower bee. The tubular flowers are unusual, in that they are pink when they first open but turn blue as they get older, providing a multi-coloured display. This native of continental Europe is an easy perennial to grow, happy in shade or in full sun. Lungwort only grows to about 25 cm, so it is best near the front of a border, or it is very useful naturalised under trees or in other shady situations where little else might grow. Clumps spread slowly and can be divided during the autumn or winter.

Honeywort****, *Cerinthe major*

An unusual annual plant from the Mediterranean. Unlike most of its relatives in this list, honeywort is slender, hairless and petite, growing to only about 60 cm. The purple flowers resemble those of comfrey, but are even more rewarding for bees, producing huge amounts of nectar that literally drips from them. The flowers appear from late May through to September. Easily grown from seed, in a well-drained position in full sun, honeywort will self-seed and persist for many years without help, but I've always found it hard to keep this plant going in my soggy clay garden.

Molktia petraea****

A compact, dense perennial, growing to about 30 cm and ideal for a well-drained situation such as a rockery. This native of the Balkans produces masses of blue tubular flowers in May and June that are hugely attractive to bumblebees. It is not easy to obtain, but can be bought from the RHS's plant shop at Wisley or by seed via mail order.

*Phacelia tanacetifolia******, blue tansy, scorpionweed

An annual plant from North America, sometimes sold as a green manure, *Phacelia* is spectacularly attractive to all sorts of short-tongued bees and hoverflies. The clusters of purple flowers produce abundant nectar and plentiful purple pollen on very long anthers that give the flowers a spiky appearance. *Phacelia* is very easy to grow from seed, germinating well and growing fast. It flowers within about eight weeks of sowing and continues to flower for another eight weeks or so. Sow seeds in autumn for early flowering the following spring, or any time though spring to early summer. If it is in a sunny spot with a little soil disturbance to provide space for germination, *Phacelia* will self-seed.

Viper's bugloss*****, *Echium vulgare*

A stunning biennial wild flower growing to about 1.5 m, flowering in July and August and absolutely loved by bees of all types for its copious nectar. Viper's bugloss likes a sunny, well-drained site. In the wild it thrives on the shingle of Dungeness and along the sides of tank tracks on the chalky soils of Salisbury Plain, helping to make these two places amongst the best sites in Britain for bumblebees. Viper's bugloss does suffer from mildew in damp weather, and during winter is prone to rotting on heavy clay soils. It is very easily grown from seed, and it will self-seed given half a chance. If you are feeling ambitious and live in a milder part of the UK, you might also try growing the giant *Echium wildpretii* or *Echium pininana* from Tenerife, both of which reach 3 m or more in height and are a huge magnet to bees.

Top to bottom:

Molktia

Phacelia

(l) Viper's bugloss

(r) Echium
wildpretii

Broomrape family, *Orobanchaceae*

An unusual family of parasitic and semi-parasitic plants that suck nutrients from the roots of their host plants. The fully parasitic species have no chlorophyll and so are not green; they only poke above ground to produce anaemic-looking flowers. Some broom-rapes found in southern Europe are major crop pests, attacking beans, tomatoes and potatoes amongst others.

Yellow rattle***, *Rhinanthus minor*

Yellow rattle is an inconspicuous wild flower, typically found in old hay meadows and in the *machair* habitat of west Scotland. In June it produces yellow flowers in which the nectar is hidden at the end of such a long tube that only long-tongued bumblebees can reach it, although buff-tailed and white-tailed bumblebees often bite holes in the sides of the flowers to rob them. However, the real value of this plant to pollinators is as a means of suppressing the growth of vigorous grasses when restoring meadows, for yellow rattle is semi-parasitic, its roots tapping in to those of the grasses. The use of yellow rattle in meadow restoration is covered in 'Creating Your Own Wildflower Meadow'. Most meadow plants are perennials, but yellow rattle is an exception: the plants die after setting seed each year, so if you wish to encourage rattle in a meadow area it is vital not to take a hay cut until after the rattle has set its seed.

Buttercup family, *Ranunculaceae*

The buttercup family includes many species, and the majority of them are not especially attractive to insects or useful in the garden, but it does contain a few gems.

*Aquilegia****, columbine, granny's bonnet

Surely everybody loves the delicate, nodding blooms of *Aquilegia*? This is a beautiful and traditional cottage-garden perennial that will grow in sun or partial shade. The nectar is hidden in long, curved tubes, and can only be reached by long-tongued bumblebee species such as the garden bumblebee, *Bombus hortorum*. However, you should keep an eye out for nectar-robbing by short-tongued species such as the buff-tailed bumblebee, *Bombus terrestris*, which will bite through the side of the tube to get to the nectar. Avoid double varieties, which are shunned by pollinators. *Aquilegia* seeds are slow to germinate but, once you have a few plants, readily self-seed. Any gardening friends who have *Aquilegia* are bound to have some spare seedlings.

Hellebore**, *Helleborus foetidus*

Hellebore, sometimes known as stinking hellebore, is an odd-looking plant up to about 40 cm tall, with shiny green leaves and clusters of nodding, purple and greenish flowers. It flowers in late winter, and so is perfectly timed for the very first emerging queen bumblebees. Hellebores prefer moderate shade, and so are useful for planting beneath orchard trees or in a dark corner of a city garden where little else might thrive. They are best grown from seed, although I find they seed themselves and pop up fairly often without my help, so I rarely need to bother actively propagating them.

Love-in-a-mist**, *Nigella damascena*

A charming and easy-to-grow annual plant originating from southern Europe, love-in-a-mist is ideal for filling a gap in a sunny herbaceous border, or for children to grow in pots on the patio. The attractive foliage is finely divided and feathery, supporting a profusion of sky-blue flowers in summer that draw a range of short-tongued bumblebees and honey bees. The seed pods are also ornamental, and

Clockwise from top:
Yellow rattle
Hellebore
Love-in-a-mist
Aquilegia

are often dried for flower arrangements. Love-in-a-mist is best prop-agated by sowing seeds in mid-spring in the places where you want them to flower.

Meadow rue***, *Thalictrum aquilegiifolium*

Meadow rue is a vigorously growing herbaceous perennial, native to continental Europe. It forms slowly spreading clumps up to about 1 m in height, and produces attractive creamy-pink clusters of fluffy-looking flowers in late spring, enjoyed by many insects but particularly popular with hoverflies. This is a useful plant as it favours damp, boggy areas with some shade, conditions that do not suit many pollinator-friendly plants. Propagate by splitting clumps in early spring, or by seed.

Cabbage family, *Brassicaceae*

The cabbage family is one of the most important plant families for humans, containing numerous crops including broccoli, cauliflower, turnip, oilseed rape and radish. If you grow any of these in the veget-able patch it is worth letting a few go to seed, for the flowers of almost all cabbage-family plants are attractive to many different species of bee, including a broad range of solitary bees such as yellow-faced bees, mining bees and sweat bees, and also hoverflies. Radish in par-ticular is very easy and quick to grow, and flowers within eight weeks of sowing. This family also includes some notorious weeds such as charlock, the yellow flowers of which are also popular with pollin-ators and make an excellent honey.

Erysimum 'Bowles Mauve'****, Perennial wallflower

Erysimum is a bushy evergreen perennial up to 80 cm tall, derived from a southern European plant, *Erysimum cheiri*. It must be a contender for the plant with the longest flowering period, for 'Bowles Mauve' can flower for almost twelve months of the year, although the clusters of purple flowers are at their most prolific in spring. It attracts numerous short-tongued bumblebees, solitary bees and butterflies. *Erysimum* grows best in a sunny, well-drained spot, and makes an attractive pot plant for patios. It tends to be quite short-lived, but is easily multiplied and replaced by taking cuttings in spring.

Crane's-bill family, *Geraniaceae*

There are a number of attractive, native crane's-bill species, gaining their name from the seed pods, which resemble the head of a stork or crane.

Geranium****, meadow crane's-bill (*Geranium pratense*) and others

The lovely, delicate flowers of geraniums are available in a wide range of colours and sizes, some little changed from the wild species from which they originate. There are varieties suitable for rockeries, herbaceous borders, naturalising in a meadow or growing in pots. Most hardy geranium species are very good for bees, but if I had to pick one I would go for the mauve flowers of the beautiful native meadow crane's-bill (*G. pratense*). In trials, *Geranium* 'Rozanne' performed best of the garden varieties, which is surprising since this is a sterile hybrid. Perhaps it can put more energy into flowering because it does not produce seed, for it certainly flowers prolifically. *Geranium sanguinea* is also good, as are the cultivated forms 'Patricia' and 'Ann Folkard'. If cut back after flowering most types will flower again, providing blooms throughout the summer. Geraniums are best propagated by dividing clumps or taking cuttings. Do not confuse them with their gaudy South African relatives the pelargoniums (often wrongly called geraniums), which are commonly grown in hanging baskets and window boxes. Pelargoniums are of little value to insects.

Clockwise from top:
Erysimum
Meadow rue
Geranium 'Rozanne'
Geranium pratense

Daisy family, *Asteraceae*

A vast plant family with more than 30,000 known species, only the orchid family rivals it for numbers (scientists cannot agree as to which is largest family). Members of the *Asteraceae* have unusual and distinctive flower heads, actually composed of hundreds of tiny flowers squeezed together. Many members of this family are excellent for insects, and some of them are also among our most familiar wild flowers, such as the daisy. Aside from those listed below, some of the best for pollinators include almost all types of thistle, and also cornflower.

Burdock***, *Arctium lappa*

Burdock is a chunky perennial wild flower growing up to 2 m tall, producing thistle-like flowers in July and August, followed by annoyingly clinging Velcro-like seed burrs. The flowers seem to be particularly attractive to common carder bumblebees, which make up the large majority of visits, presumably because their medium-length tongues are perfectly matched to the depth of the flowers. Burdock is probably a bit thuggish for growing in an ornamental border, but is a good plant for wild areas, tolerating most conditions including shade. Burdock is best grown from seeds, either sprinkled where they are to flower, or sown in seed trays – but planted out soon after germination before the taproot has developed.

Cardoon****, *Cynara cardunculus*

Cardoons and globe artichokes are different varieties of the same species, both grown primarily for culinary purposes, but in my view they are more valuable as a nectar source for bumblebees. The plants can be huge, with splendid whitish architectural foliage and huge purple flowers borne on sturdy stems over 2 m tall. They take up a lot of space, and they produce just a few huge flowers in late summer, but those flowers become absolutely smothered in bees, particularly young queen bumblebees fattening up for winter. A spectacular plant if you have space, it has the benefit that you can eat the (rather chewy) leaf stalks, or deprive the bees by picking and eating the large flower buds. Cardoons are fairly easy to grow from seed, or you can take basal cuttings in late winter.

*Centaurea scabiosa****, greater knapweed and relatives

Do not be put off by the 'weed' in the common name: knapweeds are the wild relatives of the *Centaurea* commonly sold in garden centres. They are beautiful meadow flowers that attract a host of bees and butterflies. Plants can grow quite large, and produce dozens of purple flower heads on stalks that stand about 1 m tall. They are well suited to a herbaceous border, and are also commonly included in meadow seed mixes. Most *Centaurea* are perennials, but this genus also includes cornflower (*Centaurea cyanus*), a charming annual which, along with poppies, was once a common sight in our arable fields. All are easy to cultivate from seed.

*Chrysanthemum****

I always associate *Chrysanthemum* with funerals, and the common 'double' varieties are hopeless for insects, so these plants feature on very few lists of those recommended for wildlife. Nonetheless, the old-fashioned single varieties, which provide a spectacular splash of colour in late summer and autumn, are very popular with late-season bumblebees, honey bees and hoverflies such as drone flies right into November. 'Early Yellow', 'Fred's Yellow', 'Perry's Peach', 'Nancy Perry' and 'Lady in Pink' are all varieties that are attractive to insects. *Chrysanthemum* are woody perennials, growing to about 1 m tall and with daisy-like flowers in white, pink, purple, yellow or orange. They do best in a sunny, sheltered, well-drained situation. *Chrysanthemum* are best propagated by basal cuttings or by dividing clumps.

Burdock

Cardoon

Centaurea scabiosa

Centaurea cyanus

Chrysanthemum

Cone flower

Cone flower****, *Echinacea purpurea*

A hardy, clump-forming perennial daisy from North America, growing to about 1.5 m and producing dramatic large flowers with distinctive cone-shaped centres. These are usually purple or pink, but white, yellow and red varieties are also available. Cone flower is very attractive to longer-tongued insects such as butterflies and some bumblebees. This is a splendid plant for a herbaceous border, preferring full sun but able to cope with some shade. Cone flowers can be grown from seeds sown once the weather has warmed up in mid-spring, via root cuttings or by dividing clumps.

Cosmos**, *Cosmos bipinnatus* & others

Cosmos are popular, colourful annuals originating from North America. They grow to 1 m or more and bear large pink, orange or white daisy-style flowers in profusion. Cosmos have been long-overlooked as plants for insects, for they appear on few lists of pollinator-friendly plants, but I find them to be well worth growing, drawing in a broad range of short-tongued bees and hoverflies. They are among the easiest and most colourful plants you might grow, and are ideal for beginners and children, as they can flower within seven weeks of sowing and continue until the first frosts. Sow seeds direct where they are to flower once the danger of frosts has passed, or in seed trays under glass if you want to get them going earlier in spring. Seeds are easily collected for the following year. Cosmos thrive in most soils but prefer a sunny location.

*Dahlia**** 'Bishop of Llandaff'

Dahlia feature in few lists of recommended plants for pollinators, but open varieties such as this one can be fantastic magnets for bumble-bees (avoid the 'cactus' or 'pompom' varieties, which are showy but useless). 'Bishop of Llandaff' has brilliant red flowers and purplish foliage, grows up to 1 m tall and flowers from August through to the first frosts. The tubers are sensitive to frost, so they are best dug up and stored for the winter. If you get peckish and run out of potatoes, the tubers are edible. *Dahlia* prefer a sunny position, and some of the smaller varieties such as 'Happy Single Flame' are well suited to growing in pots. Dahlia are usually purchased as tubers in later winter, but are also easy to grow from seed.

Dandelion***, *Taraxacum officinale*

In most gardening books the only mention of dandelions might be in the weed section, but they are wonderful native flowers. They provide a gorgeous flush of yellow flowers in early spring, peaking in April, a time when not too much else has begun to offer nectar, and so are much loved by a large variety of spring-flying insects. You generally don't need to give dandelions a helping hand with propagation – they do it pretty well by themselves, scattering their wind-borne seeds far and wide. My lawn is full of dandelions and, although I do spend quite a bit of the spring hoeing out the seedlings that pop up unwanted in the vegetable patch and flower beds, I wouldn't be without them. I am often saddened to see road verges and roundabouts that are bright yellow with massed dandelions one day, but by the next have been strimmed or mowed down to nothing. Similarly, it is all too common to see dandelions that have managed to gain a footing among the cracks of our city pavements being sprayed off with herbicide. Why can't we just leave them and enjoy their flowers?

Dyer's camomile***, *Anthemis tinctoria,*
also known as golden marguerite

This is a hardy but short-lived perennial plant which forms attractive green mounds of finely divided foliage up to about 70 cm tall, above which masses of cheerful lemon-yellow daisy flowers are produced from June to August. In field trials by Rosi Rollings of RosyBee Plants this came out as one of the very best plants for attracting our smaller solitary bees. Dyer's camomile thrives in a sunny, well-drained position, and is an excellent choice for growing in a pot on a balcony or patio, as it copes well with drought if you should forget to water it. It can be propagated from basal cuttings or comes up readily from seeds in spring.

French marigold*** (*Tagetes* species)

Familiar orange- and yellow-flowered plants, sadly on sale mostly in 'double' varieties, which are of little interest to insects. However, single-flowered varieties such as *Tagetes patula*, 'Disco Yellow', are very attractive to short-tongued pollinators, particularly hoverflies, and can be very useful in attracting aphid-eating hoverflies to the vegetable patch. Marigolds are also strongly aromatic, and the scent is said to deter whitefly from plants such as tomatoes – a bonus to growing them. There are both perennial and annual French marigolds, but they are usually grown as annuals, and sown as seeds in spring. They are neat, compact plants, most varieties growing up to about 30 cm tall, and they will flower from late spring until killed by frosts in autumn. Marigolds need full sun to thrive.

Globe thistle***, *Echinops spp.*

A substantial perennial plant growing up to 1.5 m tall, and so best placed at the back of a border, globe thistle is named for its striking, globe-shaped and spiky-looking, powder-blue flowers produced in high summer, which are much loved as a nectar source by bumble-bees and honey bees. Globe thistles thrive in poor, well-drained soil, and prefer a sunny position. They are easily propagated from seed or by dividing established plants in winter. Several species are available, of which *E. bannaticus*, *E. exaltatus* and *E. sphaerocephalus* are all highly attractive to bees.

Top to bottom:

(l) Cosmos (r) Dyer's camomile

(l) Dahlia 'Bishop of Llandaff'
(r) French marigold

(l) Dandelion (r) Globe thistle

Goldenrod****, *Solidago spp.*

Goldenrods are amongst the most important wild flowers for bumble-bees in North America, but only one relatively scarce species (*Solidago virgaurea*) is native to the UK. A number of garden varieties are also available, all clump-forming perennials usually growing to about 1 m tall, and producing very attractive arching sprays of tiny yellow flowers in late summer and autumn. Goldenrods are attractive to many different bees, including bumblebees, honey bees, sweat bees and nomad bees. They can thrive in very poor soil, but prefer an open situation. Propagation is easiest by dividing existing clumps.

Hawkbit, hawksbeard, hawkweed****

There are a bewildering number of very similar native plant species belonging to the genera *Leontodon, Crepis, Hieracium* and *Pilosella*, all of which have a basal rosette of more or less hairy leaves, and produce flowers on slender stalks that are very similar to dandelion but smaller. I'm lumping them all together here, so my apologies if that offends any keen botanists. They are mainly perennial meadow plants, often found growing in lawns, and they quickly send up their yellow flowers if mowing is stopped for a week or two any time between May and October.

These flowers are the mainstay of the diet of a large array of solitary bees, including various mining bees, mason bees, leafcutter bees and nomad bees. If you have them in your lawn (the prostrate rosettes of leaves are easy to spot), then simply stop mowing your lawn for a couple of weeks and they will spring into flower. On a warm day almost every flower will have one or more small solitary bees, many of them tiny, all of which have presumably been waiting patiently for you to put the mower away. Red-tailed bumblebees are also partial to these flowers. Most species readily grow from seeds, and many meadow seed mixes contain some. I encourage them by sprinkling a few seeds onto the molehills that regularly appear on my lawn and in my wildflower meadow.

Goldenrod

Hawkbit

Hemp-agrimony

Helenium

Ox-eye daisy

Michaelmas daisy

*Helenium*****, sneezewort

Originating from North America, and producing glowing, red, orange or yellow daisy-like flowers on tall stems up to 1 m, *Helenium* are a magnet for honey bees, solitary bees and hoverflies from August through to October. There are a number of species and hybrid garden varieties: 'Moerheim Beauty' is an excellent variety I have tried, while *Helenium autumnale* comes highly recommended. *Helenium* prefers a well-drained soil in full sun, and is prone to dying off in the winter in my soggy clay garden. I also find it is a favourite snack for wild rabbits, but so long as they are kept at bay it is easy to grow. Propagate by taking basal cuttings or dividing clumps. In case you are wondering, the common name 'sneezewort' derives from the former use of the dried leaves of this plant in snuff, while the Latin name is a tribute to Helen of Troy.

Hemp-agrimony***, *Eupatorium cannabinum*

A robust native perennial wild flower, growing to about 1.5 m tall and producing a mass of pinkish flower heads in late summer that are attractive to a range of insects, but particularly to butterflies. It prefers a moist and sunny site, but can survive almost anywhere. The leaves are toxic, so are avoided by rabbits. Hemp-agrimony is a great plant for a wild corner of the garden where it will look after itself. It can be grown from seed, and clumps are readily split in winter.

Michaelmas daisy***, *Aster* species

There are many different species and garden varieties of Michaelmas daisy, mostly originating from North America. They are attractive herbaceous plants, producing masses of purple, daisy-like flowers in later summer and autumn. *Aster novi-belgii* is the most commonly grown species, and it seems to be especially attractive to honey bees, whereas *A. amellus* is hugely attractive to hoverflies, particularly drone flies stocking up on food before they go into hibernation. Most asters are perennials, forming dense clumps about 1 m tall, and spreading via rhizomes. They are very easy to grow, and are easily propagated by splitting clumps in the autumn or winter. They are ideal for an herbaceous border, but can also be naturalised in wild areas.

Ox-eye daisy**, *Leucanthemum vulgare*

A fairly common perennial wild flower, typically found in hay meadows, and perfect for naturalising in wild or meadow areas or planting in an herbaceous border. Ox-eye daisy spreads slowly via rhizomes, and produces dense clumps of leaves low to the ground, from which sprout the characteristic yellow and white daisy flowers held on slender stems up to about 70 cm tall. The amounts of nectar produced are quite small, so large bees such as bumblebees don't tend to bother with ox-eye daisy, but many small solitary bees, soldier beetles and also hoverflies feed upon them. Ox-eye daisy is usually included in wild flower meadow-seed mixes, and tends to establish well from seed, although it can also be propagated by splitting clumps over the winter.

Plume thistle***, *Cirsium rivulare* '*Atropurpureum*'

A great plant for male bumblebees in high summer, this species is not spiny like its wild thistle relatives, and is quite at home in a flower bed. The rosettes of dense green leaves send up purple, nodding flower heads on stems up to 1 m tall from June to August. Plume thistle can spread vegetatively and, given half a chance, can take over more space than you intended. It is easily propagated from root cuttings.

If you have a large garden with a wild or meadow area, you might also consider letting our native thistle species have room. Creeping thistle (*Cirsium arvense*), marsh thistle (*Cirsium palustre*) and spear thistle (*Cirsium vulgare*) are all wonderful flowers for bees and butterflies, and also provide food plant for the painted lady butterfly. Marsh and spear thistle can be kept under control easily by dead-heading before the fluffy seeds blow away. Creeping thistle is more of a thug, Its name referring to the spreading rhizomes which creep along deep underground. I have all of them in my garden, although I sometimes question the wisdom of this.

Ragwort****, *Senecio jacobaea*

I am aware that by including ragwort in a list of suitable flowers for the bee-friendly garden I am inviting trouble (a red ragwort to a bull?). This plant is notorious for poisoning livestock, while Lord Tebbit once suggested that young people and criminals should be given the task of pulling ragwort as a kind of National Service. In 2007 a *Daily Mail* article quoted the British Horse Society as claiming that 6,500 horses a year die of ragwort poisoning. The article went on to claim that pulling ragwort is dangerous for humans, because the plant's toxins can be absorbed through the skin and lead to 'slow and irreversible cirrhosis' (of the liver). Cue media demands that it must be eradicated.

In reality, this is all almost complete bunkum. Grazing animals avoid eating the live plant, so it poses no danger to them. If it is present in dried hay in large quantities it can be poisonous to horses and cattle, but there have been only a handful of confirmed cases; the 6,500 figure seems to be wildly inflammatory. As for humans, there have been no known cases of poisoning. A sector of the rural community seems to have demonised this plant for little reason.

The real ragwort is a pretty, native flower that provides home and food to seventy-seven different insect species, thirty of which are entirely dependent on it. Ten of these insects are endangered. Another 117 species of insect have been recorded visiting the flowers for nectar or pollen – in my garden, it is especially popular with small copper and small skipper butterflies, but it also visited by hoverflies, bumblebees, solitary bees, soldier beetles and more. In short, ragwort is a wonderful plant for insect life.

If you need to, propagation is easy enough from wild-collected seed, and ragwort looks perfectly at home in the midst of a herbaceous border or in a meadow area.

*Rudbeckia fulgida***, black-eyed Susan

A deservedly popular herbaceous perennial, *Rudbeckia* forms robust clumps up to 1 m tall, bearing copious daisy-style flowers with chocolate-brown centres surrounded by bright yellow petals. It is very attractive to honey bees, and moderately attractive to short-tongued bumble-bees and some solitary bees. It will thrive in sun or partial shade, is not fussy with regard to soil, and flowers from the beginning of July through to the first frosts of October if it is dead-headed regularly. *Rudbeckia* is easily propagated by dividing the rhizomatous clumps, or it can be grown from seed sown in early spring.

Sunflower***, *Helianthus*

There are many species of sunflower, most native to North America. The most familiar is *Helianthus annuus,* the annual species grown mostly in slightly warmer climates than our own as an arable crop. Garden varieties of this species produce spectacular, dinner-plate-sized flowers that attract many insects, including bumblebees, honey bees and hoverflies. They are great plants for kids to grow, germinating easily from seed and growing rapidly to tower above them. Also very useful for the wildlife gardener are some of the perennial varieties, such as *Helianthus salicifolius,* which forms dense clumps and produces clusters of flowers on stalks up to about 2 m tall. I have this species naturalised in a meadow area and it looks after itself, adding a splash of colour in autumn when the meadow is otherwise largely lacking in flowers. This genus also includes Jerusalem artichoke, one of my favourite vegetables because it is so easy to grow and very tasty.

*Top row, left to right: Cirsium rivulare,
Cirsium palustre, Cirsium vulgare*

Middle: (l) Ragwort (r) Rudbeckia fulgida

*Bottom: (l) Sunflower
(r) Helianthus salicifolius*

Figwort family, *Scrophulariaceae*

Culver's root***, *Veronicastrum virginicum*

This is a splendid perennial wild flower from the eastern United States, with cream, pink or purplish flower spires up to 1.5 m tall in high summer that are very attractive to honey bees in particular. It is easy to grow and pretty robust, coping with sun or shade and dry to boggy conditions. Culver's root can be grown from seed, or by dividing clumps once they are established.

Figwort***, *Scrophularia nodosa*

Figwort is a native perennial wild flower with glossy green rosettes of leaves, and flower spikes to 1 m tall, which bear hugely unimpressive brownish-purple flowers from June through to September. Although not beautiful, the flowers are very attractive to short- and medium-tongued bumblebees, producing glistening droplets of nectar. Figwort is happy in most soils, and in sun or partial shade. It is easily grown from seed, and in my garden happily self-seeds a little bit more than I would prefer.

Foxglove****, *Digitalis purpurea*

A very familiar and beautiful cottage-garden and woodland flower, and a favourite with long-tongued bumblebees such as the garden bumblebee, *Bombus hortorum*. Some cultivated varieties produce little nectar, so it is safest to stick to the wild purple type. Foxgloves are usually biennial, flowering in their second year and producing a huge quantity of tiny brown seeds. I snap off the drying seed heads and then wander around my garden shaking them wherever I would like more foxgloves to spring up. If you have bought a packet of seeds, sow them in late spring in seed trays, to plant out in autumn. Foxgloves will grow in most conditions, being quite happy in moderate shade or sun and in almost any soil.

Mullein*, *Verbascum* species

There are various garden varieties of mullein, but I favour the native great mullein (*Verbascum thapsus*), a stately biennial that produces a flower spike up to 2.5 m tall in its second year. Mullein likes a sunny position, but is otherwise easily pleased. The yellow flowers are produced in July and August, and are visited by bumblebees and honey bees for pollen, while wool carder bees collect the white hairs from the leaves to line their nests. If you are lucky, you may also get the pretty white-, yellow-and-black-spotted caterpillars of the mullein moth nibbling the leaves. Great mullein is best propagated by seed, but I find that the plants pop up by themselves sufficiently often that I never need to worry about actively encouraging them.

*Penstemon***

Penstemon are foxglove-like perennial plants from North America. A huge number of species and garden varieties are available, in red, purple, pink, mauve or white, and varying in height from mat-forming varieties no more than 10 cm tall to towering plants over 2 m tall. They are well suited to a cottage garden or herbaceous border, producing spires of tubular flowers from mid-summer through to the autumn frosts, and particularly attracting long-tongued bumblebees. *Penstemon* are happy in sun or partial shade in most soil types, but don't like damp conditions. Many varieties are not completely hardy, and can die off in cold winters. '*Andenken an Friedrich Hahn*' is among the hardier varieties, and won the Royal Horticultural Society's Award of Garden Merit. *Penstemon* grow readily from seed and take from softwood cuttings.

(l) Culver's root
(r) Figwort

(l) Mullein
(r) Mullein moth

(l) Foxglove
(r) Penstemon

128

Purple toadflax***, *Linaria purpurea*

A native of southern Europe, purple toadflax is a very easy-to-grow perennial, producing spires of purple flowers up to about 80 cm tall from June to October. It will grow almost anywhere with a little sunshine, suiting the herbaceous border, rockeries or wilder areas. Our native toadflax, *Linaria vulgaris*, is similar but with larger, yellow flowers. Both species have deep nectar spurs, so only long-tongued bumblebees can reach the nectar by legitimate means, but robbing by short-tongued bees is common. Toadflaxes can be propagated from seed (and often seed themselves without help), or by dividing clumps or taking softwood cuttings.

Snapdragon*, *Antirrhinum majus*

Like their relative the foxglove, snapdragons are mainly visited by long-tongued bumblebees. I used to love playing with snapdragons as a child – squeeze the snout-like flowers from the side, and they snap open. Snapdragons are short-lived perennials from southern Europe, often grown as biennials, available in a wide range of colours. They thrive best in well-drained soils, and will happily grow and self-seed in the cracks in old walls. Seeds are easily collected, and can be sprinkled where they are to flower in autumn, or sown in seed trays in spring. Snapdragons can also be grown from semi-ripe cuttings taken in September.

Speedwell***, *Veronica* species

Many species and varieties of speedwell are available, including several native wild flowers, all of them herbaceous perennials that thrive in sunny positions. Most of the ornamental varieties tend to be upright, slender plants producing spires of small purple flowers up to 1 m tall, though pink and white varieties are available. They are broadly attractive to a range of short-tongued bumblebees and honey bees.

Germander speedwell (*Veronica chamaedrys*) is one of the most common of several similar low-growing native speedwells that produce masses of delicate blue flowers in May and June. It will creep along among the grasses in meadow areas and lawns, or will thrive in partial shade under shrubs and trees, providing colourful and useful ground cover. I have lots growing beneath my soft-fruit bushes. For reasons that baffle me it is often described as a weed, but why anyone would wish to get rid of it I cannot say. The small flowers are very popular with a range of bees, but particularly many of our smaller solitary bees. I commonly see the girdled mining bee (*Andrena labiata*) on mine, a small dark bee with a chestnut red abdomen.

I find the ornamental speedwells can be tricky to germinate from seed, but clumps are readily divided.

Gourd family, *Cucurbitaceae*

This family contains a great many popular vegetables, including cucumber, squash, pumpkin, melon and courgette. All of these are visited and pollinated by a range of bees, flies and beetles.

White bryony***, *Bryonia dioica*

One of the few native members of this family, white bryony is a perennial scrambling climber, often found in hedgerows. It dies down to the ground over the winter, but sprouts rapidly each spring and can grow 4 m or more. It has attractive foliage but inconspicuous green and white flowers born from June onwards. It also has attractive bright red berries which hang into winter, when they are eaten by birds. The Royal Horticultural Society website gives much advice on how to eradicate this plant, but I rather like it and the bees seem to agree. It is very popular with honey bees, early bumblebees and many solitary bees. In particular, the bryony mining bee (*Andrena florea*) collects pollen only from white bryony, and thus is entirely dependent on this one plant species, a strategy that is very unusual amongst bees. You can only expect to see this bee species if you live in the south-east of England. To propagate white bryony, sow seeds in late autumn.

Purple toadflax

Snapdragon

Speedwell

White bryony

Honeysuckle family, *Caprifoliaceae*

An odd family, seemingly comprising a miscellaneous bunch of plants that look quite dissimilar, many of which are of great interest to bees. Among those not mentioned below, but which are moderately attractive to pollinators, are snowberry (*Symphoricarpos*) and *Leycesteria*. The latter is a useful plant because the hollow woody stems are perfect for chopping into sections and bundling together to make a cheap bee hotel.

Devil's bit scabious***, *Succisa pratensis*

A pretty native wild flower, devil's bit scabious produces purple, nectar-rich flowers up to about 80 cm tall in late summer and autumn. They are much loved by the last few bumblebees of the year, and also by butterflies fattening up before winter hibernation. Oddly, in the wild it is found on both boggy, peaty soils and dry chalk grasslands. Devil's bit scabious is easy to grow from seed or from basal cuttings. It looks very handsome in a herbaceous border, or it can be naturalised in a meadow area.

Field scabious****, *Knautia arvensis*

A lovely native meadow perennial, one of my particular favourites, perfect for a cottage-garden border or meadow area. Our wild field scabious is found on chalk downland, but it seems to survive on a range of garden soils including my wet clay, so long as it gets plenty of sun. I love the powder-puff blue of the flowers, and bees, butterflies and hoverflies seem pretty keen too. Birds such as goldfinch enjoy the seeds in winter. Field scabious flowers in July and August. There are many garden strains and other species of *Knautia* available; of these, I can vouch that *Knautia macedonica* is also excellent for bees, producing dark crimson flowers over a longer flowering period that extends until the first frosts. Both species are very easy to grow from seeds, or from softwood cuttings taken in April or May.

Honeysuckle***, *Lonicera periclymenum*

There are many species and varieties of honeysuckle, but I think you can't beat our native species, with its spectacular and gloriously scented cream and red or sometimes orange flowers. Honeysuckle is a fast-growing climber that can grow up to 7 m, perfect for covering a wall, an ugly outbuilding or a dead tree. It is a woodland plant, and so copes well with shade, and it does not seem to be particular about soil type. Honeysuckles are visited by long-tongued bumblebees, and particularly by moths – drawn to the delightful floral scent which strengthens in the evening for their benefit. The soft red berries of honeysuckle are soon scoffed by birds. I find the best way to propagate honeysuckle is by layering – pinning a wayward stem to the ground until it roots, which does not take long.

Red valerian**, *Centranthus ruber*

Originating in the Mediterranean, red valerian is a woody-based perennial that is widely naturalised in the UK. It is a handsome plant up to about 1 m tall, with glossy pale green leaves and showy clusters of crimson flowers that are attractive to butterflies, day-flying moths and the longer-tongued bumblebees. The flowers are produced from June until the first frosts, but plants can become very scraggy by late summer, and respond well to being cut back hard. Red valerian likes sunny, well-drained, impoverished sites: it will happily grow out of the cracks in an old wall, and seems impervious to summer droughts, a feature that may become particularly useful in the future as our climate changes. Red valerian sprouts readily from seed. If you become very hungry, the roots are edible.

Top:
(l) Devil's bit scabious
(r) Field scabious

Middle and bottom (l):
Honeysuckle

Bottom (r):
Red valerian

Teasel***, *Dipsacus fullonum*

Teasel is a striking, tall, native biennial growing to 3m or more, a fine architectural plant for the back of a border. The rather spiky mauve flowers are enjoyed by honey bees and bumblebees, while the seeds are a favourite with goldfinches through the winter. Teasel is a trad-itional cottage-garden flower, also suited to wild areas and capable of growing in most soil types, though it does prefer to be in full sun. It sets seed fairly readily, and can take over a little bit, but the young plants are easily hoed out if you find you have more than you want.

Hydrangea family, *Hydrangeaceae*

Most hydrangeas grown in gardens are among the most useless plants for pollinators – their vast flowers are rarely visited by anything. However, do not write them off completely, as some of the less well-known species are spectacularly good plants for insects.

*Hydrangea serratifolia******

This is a slow-growing, evergreen climber from Chile and Argentina, with the potential to eventually reach 12 m or more in height. It has glossy, very large leaves and dense clusters of creamy-white flowers in July and August. There is a magnificent old specimen in the walled garden at Wakehurst Place in West Sussex which becomes alive with bees when in flower, mainly honey bees and short-tongued bumblebees. Both this and the following species will grow and flower in sun or shade, making them particularly versatile plants, excellent for covering ugly old structures. It is said that *H. serratifolia* can be cultivated from layering or softwood cuttings, but I have not tried.

*Hydrangea petiolaris***, climbing hydrangea

A native of Japan and Korea, this hydrangea is also a slow-growing, self-clinging climber, suited to sun or shade. It is much more readily obtained than the previous species, and can also grow very large, but it differs in being deciduous, and in having flowers that are much more attractive to hoverflies and other flies than they are to bees. In fact, it produces two types of flower in mixed clusters: small, fertile flowers and larger, showy white flowers that are infertile. All hydrangeas benefit from a good supply of organic matter around their roots. Propagate via layering.

Top: (l) Hydrangea serratifolia
(r) Hydrangea petiolaris

Middle: Crocus

Bottom: (l) Iris
(r) Iris pseudacorus

Iris family, *Iridaceae*

Crocus***, *Crocus vernus* and others

A very familiar garden flower, perfect for naturalising in lawns and orchards, or planting near the front of flower borders, the crocus provides welcome colour in late February and March and is an important food source for hungry queen bumblebees when they first emerge from hibernation after being asleep since the previous summer. The 'Joan of Arc' variety is among the best for bees. Crocuses will thrive best in full sun and a well-drained soil, but they tolerate a broad range of conditions. To propagate crocus, gently dig up the bulbs after flowering. You will find that each 'mother' bulb will usually have produced a few 'offsets': small side bulbs which can be separated and replanted.

*Iris***

There are nearly 300 species of iris, and most have spectacular flowers that are attractive to bees, particularly longer-tongued bumblebees such as the common carder. Sometimes male bees will sleep in the flowers at night, which gives them shelter and helps to warm them up in the morning by trapping the sun's heat. The majority of irises prefer full sun and a well-drained position, but our native yellow flag iris (*Iris pseudacorus*) prefers damp or waterlogged conditions and will happily grow in a pond. Irises are most easily propagated by dividing clumps, best done after flowering, which in most species is in late spring/early summer.

Ivy family, *Araliaceae*

A very large, mostly tropical family that contains ginseng, but with very few species that are familiar to us in the UK.

Ivy****, *Hedera helix*

Ivy is not popular with most gardeners, and wouldn't be high on many people's list of flowers for pollinators, but it should be. The small, greenish-yellow clusters of flowers that appear in September are inconspicuous, but they attract all manner of insects, including butterflies such as the peacock and red admiral, stocking up on sugar for hibernation, and also honey bees, bumblebees, solitary bees, hoverflies, wasps and beetles. It even has its own specialist solitary bee, the aptly named ivy bee (*Colletes hederae*), which was first recorded in the UK in 2001, but has now become common in the south.

Sadly, ivy is all-too-often killed or heavily cut back, preventing it from flowering and also preventing the berries from forming – these are a good winter food for many birds. If you are lucky enough to have some, try to leave it to bush out and flower. It is often claimed that it smothers trees, but I'm not convinced: it doesn't spread far enough from the trunk to shade the canopy, and the thicket it provides by growing up a tree trunk provides wonderful habitat for all sorts of insects and nest sites for many birds. In short, if you can, make room for ivy!

Knotweed family, *Polygonaceae*

This family includes some of our more problematic weeds, such as docks and the infamous Japanese knotweed, but also useful plants such as rhubarb and buckwheat. Even the much-reviled Japanese knotweed is almost entirely edible, and its flowers are attractive to bees.

Bistort***, *Persicaria bistorta*

This is a very useful vigorous perennial that will grow almost anywhere, including shady corners. It produces a lovely show of slender-stemmed, elegant flowers in late spring, up to about 70 cm. In my garden it is regularly visited by tree bumblebees and early bumblebees. Bistort is very readily propagated from fragments of rhizomes, and can be a bit invasive, so it is best planted in a place where it can be readily contained. It mingles well with *Aquilegia* in a woodland garden.

Leadwort family, *Plumbaginaceae*

An obscure plant family with very few native UK representatives, including sea lavender and thrift.

Thrift*, *Armeria maritima*

A lovely low-growing, native, perennial plant found in the wild on rocky coastal headlands, thrift forms dense hummocks of soft, thin leaves, from which the pink flowers emerge on stalks up to 15 cm in May and June. Thrift is very drought-resistant, ideal for growing in a rockery or in pots, and is perfect for windswept coastal gardens. It can be propagated from seed, via basal cuttings or by dividing clumps.

Top: (l) Bistort (r) Thrift
Middle: Hollyhock
Bottom: Musk mallow

Mallow family, *Malvaceae*

This family contains some very important crop plants, notably cacao, okra, cotton and the notoriously smelly durian fruit. It also includes some lovely cottage-garden plants that are popular with bumblebees in particular.

Hollyhock***, *Alcea rosea*

A classic cottage-garden plant, imported from China perhaps 500 years ago. Hollyhocks are giant biennials growing to 3 m tall, and very popular with buff-tailed bumblebees. Bees seem to go for the nectar but ignore the plentiful pollen, often becoming smothered in it but making no effort to groom it into their pollen baskets. The tall flower stems need staking or growing in dense clumps, as otherwise they tend to get blown over. Hollyhocks are one of the many cultivated plant species for which 'double'-petalled varieties are available; these are of little interest to bees. Hollyhocks are easily grown from seed, although they are a little prone to slug damage as young plants.

Musk mallow***, *Malva moschata*

Musk mallow is a handsome, native, clump-forming perennial plant producing plentiful, showy pink or white flowers on stems up to about 60 cm tall from June to September. The flowers are attractive to both short-tongued bumblebees and honey bees. *Malva alcea* is a related, taller species from southern Europe, growing to 120 cm tall. Like many other members of this family, it does tend to flop over, so is best supported. Both species prefer a sunny position, but are otherwise easy to grow. Musk mallow is most easily propagated from softwood cuttings in spring or from seed.

Mint family, *Lamiaceae*

The mint family is vast, containing many wild flowers, herbs and ornamentals, including lavender, sage, thyme, marjoram, dead-nettles, hyssop and rosemary. Many of them have strongly aromatic leaves when crushed, which is why they are used in cooking. A distinctive characteristic of this family is that the stems are usually square in section, which you can feel if you roll them between your thumb and forefinger.

Black horehound**, *Ballota nigra*

Sometimes known as black stinking horehound, because the pungent smell of the crushed leaves is not pleasant, this native wild flower doesn't sound very nice, but it has reasonably attractive spikes of small purple flowers up to about 80 cm tall, and bumblebees love it. The first shrill carder bumblebee (*Bombus sylvarum*) I ever saw (a very rare species) was feeding on this, on Salisbury Plain. Black horehound is perfect for a wild area or a herbaceous border. It grows readily from seed, or one can divide existing clumps.

Bugle***, *Ajuga reptans*

Bugle is a low-growing, native perennial wild flower, also available in a number of garden varieties. It is happy in shade or sun, and is a nice creeping groundcover plant for naturalising under trees and shrubs. It flowers from May to July, producing purple, tubular flowers that are attractive to both long- and short-tongued bumblebees. Bugle is a particular favourite of the fringe-horned mason bee (*Osmia pilicornis*), a rare species confined to the south-east of England. It is most easily propagated from the many runners it produces, which readily root.

Top: (l) Black horehound
(r) Bugle

Middle: Caryopteris x clandonensis

Bottom: Catmint

*Caryopteris x clandonensis***

A large, bushy perennial growing to about 1 m, and bearing profuse mauve flowers in summer. Variety 'Heavenly Blue' seems to be particularly good for both bumblebees and honey bees and, if you are very lucky, it might attract a hummingbird hawk moth. This is a plant that really likes to be in full sun, ideally in a well-drained south-facing bank or against a south-facing wall. It is best propagated from softwood cuttings.

Catmint*****, *Nepeta racemosa* and others

If I could only grow one type of flower in my garden, I think this would be it. Catmint is a fantastic cottage-garden classic, one of the best all-round garden plants for bees of a wide range of species. Somehow its gently sprawling, soft blue flowers manage to attract both long- and short-tongued bumblebees. It is very easy to grow almost anywhere, with a long flowering period from late May through to the end of summer. No garden should be without some.

Catmints are natives of southern Europe and Asia, where there are more than 250 species. *N. racemosa* is one of the best, a sprawling, robust perennial plant, with lilac flowers through late spring to late summer. *N. x faasenii,* 'Six Hills Giant', is especially good for long-tongued bees. Many *Nepeta* varieties are currently being trialled by the Royal Horticultural Society at Wisley, and the most attractive to bees are 'Hills Grounds', 'Early Bird', 'Chettle Blue', *N. racemosa,* 'Walkers Low' and, best of all, *Nepeta grandiflora* 'Zinser's Giant'.

Catmints root very rapidly from softwood cuttings, or can be grown from seed.

Top: (l) Giant hyssop (r) Ground ivy

Middle: (l) Hedge woundwort
(r) Marsh woundwort

Bottom: (l) Lamb's ear (r) Hyssop

146

Giant hyssop*****, *Agastache*, also known as anise hyssop

One of the very best plants for bees, giant hyssop is a clump-forming perennial originally from North America. I have found it very hard to get seeds to germinate, and plants have a habit of dying over the winter on my heavy clay soil, so generally this is not a plant for the beginner. However, the bees do absolutely love it and, when thriving on a well-drained soil, it forms very attractive clumps of tall blue flower spikes up to 1 m tall in late summer. Variety 'Blackadder' seems particularly good, also 'Blue Fortune' and 'Blue Boa'. I find that the easiest way to propagate giant hyssop is from semi-ripe cuttings taken in August.

Ground ivy***, *Glechoma hederacea*

A native perennial plant, ground ivy is an evergreen, low-growing, creeping plant, great for ground cover in sun or partial shade. In the wild it often grows in hedge bottoms, and it is excellent for growing under ornamental shrubs like roses. The small blue or purple flowers are born in May and are attractive to both long- and short-tongued bees, particularly the hairy-footed flower bee and its extremely rare relative the potter flower bee, *Anthophora retusa*. Ground ivy is easily propagated by dividing clumps or from softwood cuttings.

Hedge woundwort***, *Stachys sylvatica*

Hedge woundwort is a fairly common native perennial, typically found in hedge bottoms, scrubland and woodland edges. It spreads via underground runners, and will gently increase through shady habitats without ever taking over. The whorls of small purple flowers, borne on spikes up to 60 cm in late spring and summer, are not dramatic, but this plant is very popular with carder bumblebees in particular. Hedge woundwort is not widely available as seed, but can be obtained from specialist suppliers, or just collect a few seeds from your local hedgerow. Also consider growing its relative, marsh woundwort (*Stachys palustris*) which, as the name suggests, is an ideal plant for damp areas. Betony (*Stachys officinalis*) is also an attractive meadow plant worth including in a meadow-creation seed mix.

A relative of our native woundworts, lamb's ear, *Stachys byzantina,* originates in Turkey and Iran, and is also well worth growing. The plant is entirely covered in dense white hairs, an adaptation to living in arid conditions, but nonetheless seems to grow quite well in our damp climate so long as it has a sunny position; the only difficulty I encounter is that my turkeys like to eat it. Lamb's ear is a slow-growing, spreading perennial, producing small purple flowers which are attractive to bumblebees. However, the real reason I grow it is not for the flowers or to feed the poultry, but to attract wool carder bees (*Anthidium manicatum*), large and pretty solitary bees which visit the plants to harvest the woolly hairs, which they use in their nesting burrows. Male wool carder bees are fiercely aggressive, defending patches of lamb's ear and sometimes other flowers and driving away much larger insects. They allow only female wool carders to visit their territory, and in exchange they expect to be allowed to mate. Lamb's ear is easily propagated by taking cuttings of small sections of the lower stem in spring, which readily root.

Hyssop**, *Hyssopus officinalis*

An understated, low-growing perennial herb from southern Europe, producing an abundance of small purple flowers in July and August that are highly attractive to honey bees and short-tongued bumblebees. Hyssop can also be used in cooking, and is a regular ingredient in Middle Eastern cuisine, but I must admit it is not to my taste – I prefer to leave it to the bees. It prefers a sunny, well-drained position, and is ideal for the front of a herbaceous border, in a rockery, or in a pot. Hyssop can be grown from softwood cuttings or via seeds.

Lavender****, *Lavandula*

A must for every garden, this stately mauve-flowered perennial is one of the best plants to grow if you want to guarantee a nectar supply in July and August for a range of bees, moths and butterflies. Outside my house in France I have an old lavender bush that always attracts hummingbird hawkmoths, and occasionally brings in a glorious yellow-and-black-striped swallowtail butterfly.

Lavender has a fairly long flowering period, and is available in a range of varieties and sizes. I find lavender is slow to germinate from seed, but it is very readily available as potted plants and takes fairly easily from hardwood cuttings. It does best in a sunny situation and a well-drained soil, but is otherwise pretty robust, though susceptible to very hard frosts. In the right location lavender can be long-lived, eventually developing a characterful gnarled and twisted stem. Being drought-tolerant, lavender grows very well in containers.

There are many different types of lavender available, and it pays to choose carefully. Dutch lavender, *Lavandula x intermedia*, is the best species for bee visits, and variety 'Gros Bleu' performed best of all in trials at Sussex University. The more common English lavender (*L. angustifolia*) is less attractive to pollinators, and Spanish lavender (*L. stoechas*) is worse still (though this is all relative, as they all attract quite a few insects).

English lavender   *Spanish lavender*

Lesser calamint   *Marjoram*

Lesser calamint*****, *Calamintha nepeta*

A native of southern Europe, calamint is an understated, aromatic perennial herb growing to about 60 cm, and bearing loose clusters of small white or pale pink flowers from early summer to autumn. It may not look particularly impressive, but it is much loved by all types of bee; according to trials by Rosi Rollings of rosybee nursery, this plant attracted more bees than any other of the seventy or more bee-friendly plants she has grown. Calamint is an easy-to-grow perennial, preferring a well-drained position if possible, and, being drought-resistant, it is suited to growing in pots or in a rockery. It can be readily propagated from seeds, division of clumps, or via softwood cuttings.

Marjoram*****, *Origanum vulgare*

Marjoram is a great all-rounder, very easy to grow, attractive to heaps of different pollinators, and good for cooking too. It seems to be particularly attractive to butterflies, perhaps even more so than buddleia – in my garden it often attracts gatekeepers and common blue butterflies. Marjoram is a tough perennial native, growing to about 80 cm tall, and it loves a sunny position. It is fine in a flower border, naturalised among grasses, or in a pot near the kitchen door to be handy for picking sprigs of leaves for cooking. Avoid the golden and variegated garden varieties, which in my experience are not quite as good for insects. *Origanum onites* is a similar slightly more compact and drought-tolerant species from south-east Europe that is very good for growing in containers, and is said by some to be even more attractive to bees. Marjoram takes easily from softwood cuttings made in early summer, or you can sow seeds in early spring.

Mint**, *Mentha* spp.

There are several wild species of mint in the UK and many garden varieties, all of them spreading herbaceous perennials. All are useful in cooking and for tea. Water mint (*Mentha aquatica*) is great for ponds, and is one of the most attractive mints for bees. Apple mint (*Mentha suaveolens*) is one of the tallest and most robust, growing to about 90 cm.

Most mints flower between July and September, and the flowers are attractive to bumblebees, honey bees and solitary bees. They are very easy to grow, but can be invasive, spreading via rhizomes, so if you don't want them to keep popping up further and further from where you planted them then the safest option is to plant them in containers. Mints are easily grown from softwood cuttings. They naturalise nicely in semi-wild or meadow areas, and the smell if you cut the hay is glorious.

*Monarda****, bee balm, bergamot

An elegant, showy, herbaceous perennial, originating from the prairies of North America. *Monarda* forms spreading clumps, and sends up flowering stems to about 1 m tall in summer which bear unusual whorls of red tubular flowers at the tip. In North America this plant is often visited by hummingbirds, while in the UK it is favoured by long-tongued bumblebees. It really needs a sunny, well-drained position. Monarda can be propagated by splitting clumps, by softwood cuttings or from seed, although I find germination to be slow and erratic.

*Phlomis***

Phlomis are substantial, shrubby, perennial herbs originating in the Mediterranean and Asia, needing a sunny position but able to thrive in impoverished soils. They grow to about 1.5 m tall and wide, bearing large, softly hairy leaves and whorls of attractive yellow or mauve flowers at intervals up the square stems during July and August. The flowers are deep and tubular, and so attract mostly our longest-tongued bumblebee, the garden bumblebee (*B. hortorum*). Several species are available, but I can vouch for *Phlomis samia* as attracting a steady stream of bees. *Phlomis* are most easily propagated via semi-ripe cuttings taken in July or August.

*Salvia****, including sage (*Salvia officinalis*), meadow clary (*Salvia pratensis*) and many others

Many garden salvias are available, but I love meadow clary (*S. pratensis*), an elegant and beautiful perennial wild flower with spikes of mauve flowers in June and July. This rare native meadow plant is worth growing just to observe the pollination mechanism: when a bee probes for nectar, this triggers the stamens to curl down and deposit a blob of pollen onto the bee's back. *Salvia x sylvestris* 'Indigo' is a handsome garden variety, with indigo-purple flowers that bees adore. Most salvias do best in full sun, but woodland sage, *Salvia nemorosa,* a native of Central Europe, is great for partially shaded positions. Common sage (*S. officinalis*) is particularly popular with long-tongued bees, and of course is also a versatile herb in the kitchen. Salvias are most easily propagated via semi-ripe cuttings in late summer (for larger-leaved varieties) or via softwood cuttings in spring (for smaller-leaved varieties).

Skullcap***, *Scutellaria galericulata*

A native perennial herb growing to about 60 cm in height, this is a plant best suited to damp situations. It can also cope with partial shade. Skullcap bears dense clusters of tubular, mauve flowers from June to September, which almost exclusively attract garden bumblebees, *B. hortorum*. It can be propagated by dividing clumps in early spring, from seeds sown in late spring, or from basal cuttings taken in June.

Top: (l) Water mint (r) Monarda

Middle: Salvia + Broad bordered bee hawk

Bottom: (l) Phlomis (r) Skullcap

153

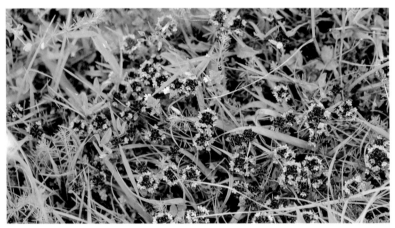

Top: (l) Rosemary (r) Rosemary beetle
Middle: Thyme
Bottom: White dead-nettle

Rosemary***, *Rosmarinus officinalis*

Rosemary is a woody, perennial herb from the Mediterranean, which is usually grown for its needle-like, fragrant, evergreen leaves, that have many uses in cooking. Rosemary is an odd plant, in that it flowers almost all year round, including in the depths of winter, providing a splash of blue when nothing much else is out. It tends to flower most in early spring, and is popular with both early-spring bumblebee queens and also bee flies (*Bombylius*). So long as it is in a well-drained position rosemary is pretty tough and easy to grow. It is particularly well adapted to cope with drought, needing no water even in the driest summers, an attribute that may prove very useful in a future of warming climates and expensive water. The easiest way to propagate rosemary is via softwood cuttings, which root very readily. If you are lucky, your rosemary will be attacked by rosemary beetles, gorgeous metallic-green and purple insects which some heathens might consider to be pests.

Thyme***, *Thymus polytrichus* subsp. *Britannicus*

There are a number of wild and cultivated species of thyme, but this one is perhaps the best for pollinators. As well as bumblebees, thyme also attract hoverflies and honey bees in abundance to its clusters of small purple flowers. This is a lovely, low-growing, rambling perennial plant for a pot, the cracks in a patio, a rockery, or in the front of a border. Thyme prefers a sunny, well-drained position, and is tolerant of drought. It is easily propagated via a range of methods: from seed sown in spring, via softwood cuttings in early summer, or by division of plants over the winter.

White dead-nettle***, *Lamium album*

White dead-nettle is a native perennial wild flower often found in hedge bottoms. It forms spreading clumps, and the flowers are an absolute favourite with common carder bee (*Bombus pascuorum*) and garden bumblebee (*Bombus hortorum*) queens in the spring. It often has a second flush of flowering later in the year. In a flower garden white dead-nettle can take over a bit, but it is a great plant for semi-wild areas or under orchard trees, where it will tolerate moderate shade. It is easily propagated from seed, softwood cuttings or by dividing clumps.

Wood sage**, *Teucrium scorodonia*

A native, clump-forming perennial growing to about 70 cm in height, wood sage bears inconspicuous greenish-yellow flowers in July and August. It is a plant of sandy soils, found in the wild in sand dunes and woodland and on heaths, and is thus a useful plant if your garden is sandy and shaded, conditions that few other plant species will enjoy. Although not showy, the flowers attract medium- and long-tongued bumblebees such as the common carder, and also honey bees. Other, prettier species and varieties of *Teucrium* are available from garden centres, including hedge germander, *Teucrium x lucidrys*, which I find is also very attractive to bumblebees and produces its pink flowers from June to October. This plant is tolerant of drought, and is ideal for a rockery or growing in a pot. *Teucrium hircanicum* is also very attractive, with purple flower spikes in late summer that are liked by honey bees. *Teucrium* grow readily from softwood cuttings.

Nasturtium family, *Tropaeolaceae*

An obscure group of plants from South America, some of which were brought back to Europe 500 years ago by Spanish explorers.

Nasturtium**, *Tropaeolum majus*

Nasturtiums are sprawling, low-growing, half-hardy annual plants, suitable for planting in pots and rockeries or at the front of herbaceous borders. Given a sunny, well-drained position they can grow very fast. Nasturtiums produce dramatically bright-orange flowers from mid-summer until the first frosts. The flowers hide their nectar in a long tube where only the very longest-tongued bumblebees can reach it, such as the garden bumblebee and its rare relative the ruderal bumblebee (*Bombus ruderatus*). Buff- and white-tailed bumblebees sometimes bite holes to rob the nectar. The flowers are also edible with a peppery taste, adding a bit of colour and spice to salads, while unripe seed pods can be pickled in vinegar to make a substitute for capers. Sow nasturtium seeds outdoors in April where they are to flower. Nasturtiums seem to be very popular with blackfly, and are sometimes grown to draw blackfly away from bean crops.

Onion family, *Amaryllidaceae*

This family includes daffodils and snowdrops, but the ones of most interest to pollinators all belong to one genus, *Allium*, which includes several familiar and useful plants, such as onions, garlic, chives and leeks.

*Allium****, including chives, leeks, and ornamental varieties

Many large and showy alliums are sold as garden ornamentals, and most are popular with both bumblebees and solitary bees. For example, *Allium hollandicum* is widely available, producing large, round, purple flower heads from May to July. Some of these ornamental alliums are huge (up to 2 m), and are most impressive at the back of a herbaceous border.

Other less flamboyant species of *Allium* are also well worth growing. I recently discovered Sicilian honey garlic, *Allium siculum*, via a tip-off on social media. It is well named, for it produces rather odd, pendent cream-and-magenta flowers that in early summer literally drip with nectar. Despite being from southern Europe, they seem to thrive in my garden, where they are particularly favoured by red-tailed bumblebees. The related lady's leek (*Allium cernuum*) from North America is also very pretty, with clusters of pink, bell-shaped flowers that are highly attractive to a range of short-tongued bumblebees.

Chives (*Allium schoenoprasum*) is a traditional cottage-garden herb, the leaves being excellent when mixed into an omelette. The pretty pink flowers appear in mid-spring and are a favourite with early bumblebees among others. It grows well in almost any soil so long as it gets some sunshine, or will thrive in a pot on the patio.

Leeks (*Allium ampeloprasum*) are also worth growing for their flowers. You may be surprised to see the humble leek appearing in a list of the best bee-friendly flowers, but I think its value has been overlooked. Leeks are normally harvested in the autumn or winter of the year in which they are sown, but if you leave a few in the ground they will reward you with huge, globular flower heads in mid-summer. These are very popular with a range of insects, including solitary bees, bumblebees and butterflies. In my garden they seem to be particularly attractive to comma butterflies, which are among our most beautiful insects.

Allium generally thrive best in a sunny, well-drained position, and do not like waterlogged ground in winter. The ornamental varieties are widely available as bulbs, best planted in the autumn or late winter. Once established they can be dug up and 'offsets' – small side bulbs – removed and planted separately. Leeks and chives are both exceedingly easy to grow from seeds sown in early spring.

Clockwise from top left: Allium hollandicum, Sicilian honey garlic, Lady's leek, Leek, Chive, Garlic chive

Peony family, *Paeoniaceae*

Very popular, classic, herbaceous perennials, with vast, blowsy flowers in red or cream, peonies are most commonly grown in double forms that are absolutely useless for pollinators. Oddly, honey bees seem attracted to the flower buds, which seem to exude a sweet liquid. Even single varieties of peony are generally of little interest to most insects, but the one below, by contrast, is great.

*Paeonia peregrina*****

I discovered this plant in the Royal Horticultural Society's garden at Wisley, where it was being absolutely mobbed by honey bees and bumblebees. Some of the large magenta flowers had as many as ten bees crammed into them – I have rarely seen anything like it. The plants grow to about 80 cm tall and wide, and bear plenty of flowers in late May and June. Propagation is not easy: the best option is to buy a plant and then divide it in winter.

Passion vine family, *Passifloraceae*

This is a large family of mainly tropical vines, some of which are grown commercially for the fruits. Almost all have gorgeous, exotic blooms that produce copious nectar and attract bumblebees, honey bees and, in warmer climes, also bats and hummingbirds.

Blue Passion Flower***, *Passiflora caerulea*

This is one of the hardiest of the passion vines, able to survive down to -10°C, and therefore able to survive in most of Britain. Blue passion flower is a fast-growing, semi-evergreen climber that produces abundant tendrils; it is self-clinging so long as there is something for it to grip. It can reach 14 m in height, so may need cutting back to prevent it taking over. Grow in sun or partial shade up a wall or fence, or it is great for covering a dead tree. Passion flowers take easily from softwood cuttings or from layering.

Pea family, *Fabaceae*

The pea family includes many wild flowers that are loved by bees, such as clovers, vetches, medicks and trefoils. Many of them naturally live in nutrient-poor grasslands like traditional hay meadows and downland, where their ability to fix nitrogen from the air via bacteria that live within nodules in their roots gives them an edge over other plant species. The pollen in legumes tends to be high in protein, which might be one of the reasons legume flowers are often preferred by bumblebees. Despite containing numerous species, the pea family is not strongly represented among ornamental flowers for the garden (though of course many types of peas and beans are grown in the vegetable patch).

Bird's-foot trefoil***, *Lotus corniculatus*

Also known as bacon-and-eggs, after its yellow flowers tinged with red in the middle, bird's-foot trefoil gets its name from the arrangement of the three or four seed pods, which together resemble the foot of a bird. Bird's-foot trefoil is a pretty, low-growing plant with a very long flowering period, from June to September. It is common in the wild, in meadows and road verges. It can also be planted into a lawn where, like white clover, it can survive mowing by creeping along at ground level, popping up to flower whenever mowing is paused. Bird's-foot trefoil can also look great in a rockery or border. As well as attracting bees, the leaves provide food for caterpillars of the common blue butterfly and for burnet moths, spectacular magenta-and-oily-black-winged, day-flying moths. Bird's-foot trefoil is easily grown from seed.

Bush vetch***, *Vicia sepium*

A member of the pea family, this unobtrusive, native, climbing perennial carries small purple flowers through late spring and summer and is constantly alive with the hum of carder bees. I let it ramble through a hedge, and clamber about in the herbaceous border. The large seeds are fairly easy to germinate, or clumps can be split at any time of year.

Canary clover****, *Lotus hirsutus*

A small, compact, evergreen shrub with soft, hairy leaves that grows wild on the sand dunes of Portugal, where it is very attractive to native *Anthidium* bees and honey bees. It also grows well in my garden in the UK, producing clusters of cream-coloured pea flowers in June and July, and attracting mainly bumblebees. Despite its origins, this species seems quite hardy, given a sunny position. I have grown it from seeds sown in mid-spring, and it will also take from semi-ripe cuttings. This attractive plant is not widely available, but is well worth growing if you can find some.

Clover, red or white****, *Trifolium pratense* and *Trifolium repens*

Outside of gardens, clovers are often the single most important forage plants for bumblebees. In the past they were very widely used as ley crops – breaks in an arable rotation used to boost soil fertility – and it is said that in the nineteenth and twentieth centuries clovers accounted for about three-quarters of the entire UK honey harvest. Clovers are still sometimes included in pasture-seed mixes, so both species remain fairly common in the countryside, but they are nowhere near as abundant as they once were. Red clover in particular is a great favourite with many of the really rare bumblebee species, which tend to have long tongues, such as the great yellow (*Bombus distinguendus*) and short-haired bumblebees (*Bombus subterraneus*), as well as some common ones like the garden bumblebee. It is not particularly showy as a garden plant, although it will grow well enough in a border. However, red clover is probably best used in a meadow area that is only mowed once or twice a year.

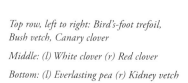

*Top row, left to right: Bird's-foot trefoil,
Bush vetch, Canary clover*

Middle: (l) White clover (r) Red clover

Bottom: (l) Everlasting pea (r) Kidney vetch

White clover is a lower-growing plant, and can survive well in regularly mown lawns; unless your lawn was recently laid it is very likely that you have some. However, mowing needs to be relaxed if it is to flower, so save yourself petrol and energy, and let the flowers in your lawn bloom. White clover is very attractive to shorter-tongued bumblebees and honey bees. Both clovers are easily grown from seed. I often sprinkle their seeds onto molehills in my meadow area and lawn, where they take readily.

Everlasting pea***, *Lathyrus latifolius*

Everlasting pea is a charming, scrambling climber that can grow up to about 3 m, and produces large, pink, pea-type flowers from late July onwards. It is particularly attractive to long-tongued bumblebees such as the garden bumblebee, and also to carpenter bees (very rare in the UK at present, but becoming more common as it warms). Unlike sweet peas, which it closely resembles, everlasting pea is a perennial and, to my mind, much easier to look after. It will grow readily from seed, and thrives in most soils in sun or partial shade. Everlasting pea looks great when sprawling through shrubs such as roses.

Kidney vetch****, *Anthyllis vulneraria*

Kidney vetch is an unobtrusive, low-growing plant with clusters of deep yellow flowers in June. It isn't often planted specifically to encourage bees but, when grown alongside clovers and trefoils, it attracts far more bumblebees than they do. If you live in the southern half of the UK and grow this plant you may be very lucky and also attract Britain's smallest butterfly and one of my absolute favourites, the gorgeous small blue. The caterpillars of this butterfly feed on the developing seed heads. This butterfly is so small that just a few plants of kidney vetch can support a sizeable colony. Kidney vetch is very easy to grow from seed.

Lupin**, *Lupinus polyphyllus*

Lupins are a lovely, traditional, cottage-garden, herbaceous perennial. The tall spires of pink, purple, yellow or white pea-like flowers
look wonderful in a herbaceous border. Most varieties produce little
nectar, but bumblebees like the bright orange pollen. Flowering
begins in late June, and can be induced to continue until August
with regular dead-heading. In Scandinavia lupins are widely regarded
as an invasive weed, but thankfully they do not seem to be a problem
in the UK. They are short-lived plants, prone to aphid outbreaks and
dying off in winter, but they are easily propagated from seed and will
seed themselves if you go easy on the dead-heading.

Meadow vetchling***, *Lathyrus pratensis* in Scandinavia

A sprawling, native, climbing plant, often found in meadows on
neutral and slightly acid soils. Meadow vetchling produces yellow,
pea-type flowers from May to August, and is much favoured by
medium- and long-tongued bumblebees, with common carder
bumblebees tending to be the most abundant visitors. It is also a
favourite food plant of the rare long-horned bee (*Eucera longicornis*),
so-named because the males have hugely elongate antennae. Meadow
vetchling is a bit messy for ornamental borders, so is probably best
reserved for meadows and wild corners of the garden. The seeds are
slow to germinate, but fragments of rhizome readily root and sprout.

Tufted vetch***, *Vicia cracca*

A really attractive climbing, scrambling, native plant that can be
grown at the back of a border and allowed to clamber up the flower
spikes of other plants or climb through a hedge. Alternatively, it is
ideal for wild areas, or spring-cut meadow areas, where it will climb
about among grass tussocks. Tufted vetch produces spikes of deep,
tubular, purple flowers from June through to September, which are

much-loved by long-tongued bumblebees. If you happen to live in the Outer Hebrides or Orkney, this species is highly attractive to the great yellow bumblebee, one of our rarest bee species. Tufted vetch is readily grown from seed.

Top: (l) Lupin
(r) Meadow vetchling

Middle: Tufted vetch

Bottom: (l) Sainfoin
(r) Wisteria frutescens

Sainfoin**, *Onobrychis viciifolia*

A favourite of mine, sainfoin produces vivid spikes of pink flowers up to about 60 cm tall from late June to August. There is some debate as to whether this species is truly native, for it has been used as a fodder crop for thousands of years (although is little used now), and hence may have been introduced by early visitors. It is quite rare in the wild, but on some remote parts of Salisbury Plain it is common, forming a gorgeous pink carpet of flowers in summer that sways gently in the breeze. Some of the agricultural varieties of sainfoin are now very rare, and merit conservation in the same way as do rare breeds of cow or sheep. As a grassland plant, sainfoin is perhaps best grown with clovers in a meadow area, but it also looks beautiful in a flower border or rockery. Growing sainfoin from seed is straightforward.

Wisteria**, *Wisteria sinensis* and others

How can you not love wisteria? It is one of the most beautiful climbing plants, with long, cascading tresses of purple or white flowers in spring. Wisteria is a woody plant that can be grown free-standing, but it is at its best when trained up a south-facing wall or over a pergola. It can also be allowed to ramble up trees, and can reach 10 m or more. Wisteria is easily propagated by layering, or will take from either softwood or hardwood cuttings. Don't try to grow it from seed as, oddly, the plants take decades to flower when propagated this way.

In general, I am not a big fan of pruning, and think it can be a waste of time on many plants, but for wisteria it is important if you want lots of flowers. Cut new growth back to about six leaves in summer after flowering has finished, and cut back again to three to four buds in winter.

Wisteria frutescens is also worth considering: it has numerous small, purple flower clusters, and seems to be more attractive to bumblebees than the more commonly grown *W. sinensis*.

Phlox family, *Polemoniaceae*

A small plant family whose best known representative in the garden is *Phlox*, a genus that isn't especially attractive to bees.

Jacob's ladder**, *Polemonium caeruleum*

This is a very pretty little perennial, cottage-garden plant, up to 80 cm tall, often overlooked as a plant for bees. It is a rare native wild flower, usually found on limestone scree slopes, although garden escapes often turn up in other habitats like hedgerows. It is easy to grow, forming clumps that send up purple or white flowers with prominent yellow anthers in May and June. Jacob's ladder tolerates most soil conditions, and will thrive in sun or partial shade. It can be grown from seeds sown in spring, or by dividing clumps.

Pink family, *Caryophyllaceae*

A family that contains many unobtrusive little wild flowers, such as stitchwort and chickweed, and also pinks, carnations and campions.

Red campion**, *Silene dioica*

A lovely perennial, native wild flower with a very long flowering period, from May to September, this is a plant I have a real soft spot for. It will grow in sun or complete shade, and will happily look after itself in a shady corner or wild area. It is visited mainly by the long-tongued garden bumblebee, and is also a food plant for several species of moth, such as the aptly named campion moth, the caterpillars of which live inside the seed pod and eat the seeds. Unusually, plants are either male or female, and the moth wisely knows to lay its eggs only on female plants. Red campion is very easy to grow from seed and, so long as you have both male and female plants, it will seed itself freely given half a chance.

Closely related native plants also worth considering are white campion, *Silene latifolia* (which attracts moths), and ragged robin, *Silene flos-cuculi* (a pretty plant with tattered pink flowers that is well suited to damp areas).

Poppy family, *Papaveraceae*

California poppy***, *Eschscholzia californica*

California's state flower is one of the easiest plants to grow from seed, great for beginner gardeners, and produces vivid orange flowers in profusion over a very long flowering period. Unusually for a perennial it flowers very quickly from seed, and self-seeds readily. It likes a sunny, well-drained spot, and can grow happily in the poorest, stoniest soils. California poppy is best grown by sowing seeds directly where you want it to flower.

*Dicentra***, bleeding heart

Dicentra has unusual heart-shaped, blood-red flowers dangling from curving stems that attract a range of bumblebees in late spring. It is a clump-forming, low-growing plant, well suited to a herbaceous border, a rockery, or for growing in partial shade under shrubs such as roses. I find *Dicentra* hard to propagate from seed, but clumps can be split in winter.

Poppy***, *Papaver*

Our native common poppy (*Papaver rhoeas*) is familiar to all, its red, silky, tissue-soft flowers once very common in cereal fields, and famous for blanketing the battlefields of Flanders during and after the First World War. It is an annual plant, best grown by sowing seeds in autumn where you want them to flower (they germinate better if exposed to frosts over the winter). Sprinkle the seeds on disturbed ground and expect a glorious display of red the following year. Bumblebees like to collect the jet-black pollen, often buzzing their flight muscles to shake the pollen loose.

Poppy seeds are commonly mixed with the seeds of other 'arable weeds' such as cornflower and corn marigold to produce a colourful display of annual plants, but you will need to scarify or dig over the ground each autumn if you want them to come back each year, as these plants need open ground to thrive. Alternatively, grow the perennial oriental poppy (*Papaver orientale*), a clump-forming cottage-garden plant with huge floppy blooms in red, cream or white (avoiding the double varieties). If you live in the wetter west of Britain, the native perennial Welsh poppy *Papaver cambricum* is an excellent choice, bearing vivid lemon-yellow flowers over a long flowering period from late spring to autumn. All of these species produce seeds in great abundance which can be used in baking, particularly sprinkled on bread. Propagation is easy from seed, or oriental poppy can be multiplied by taking root cuttings.

This page: Poppy (Papaver rhoeas)

Left, top:
(l) California poppy (r) Dicentra

Left, bottom:
(l) Papaver orientale (r) Welsh poppy

Primrose family, *Primulaceae*

Gooseneck loosestrife***, *Lysimachia clethroides*

A very easy-to-grow, clump-forming perennial from China, growing about 1 m tall and producing elegant white flower spikes with a characteristic swan-necked curve from June to August. This species likes a moist position, but is otherwise unfussy and fast-growing, perfect for a herbaceous border. I find that gooseneck loosestrife is one of the best plants for attracting butterflies, particularly browns such as gatekeepers and ringlets. It is also attractive to hoverflies and bumblebees. Clumps are very easily divided in autumn or winter.

Primrose*, *Primula vulgaris*

A familiar and still reasonably common perennial wild flower, often seen in hedge-banks and woodland edges. Primrose never attracts large numbers of pollinators, but it is liked by queen common carder bumblebees, bee flies and hairy-footed flower bees. The delicate, butter-centred, pale-yellow flowers, usually produced from late March onwards, are a welcome sign that spring is underway. Many hybrids and varieties are available in a range of colours, some of them flowering through the winter months, but to my mind you can't beat the native type. They are low-growing, shade-tolerant plants suited to wild and woodland areas, naturalising among grass, or rockeries. Primrose are best propagated from seed, sown on the surface of compost in seed trays in summer or autumn. The related cowslip (*Primula veris*) is also beautiful, and is propagated in the same way. It attracts a similar range of insects, though it is less shade-tolerant than primrose and is best planted in full sun in a meadow area or on a south-facing bank.

Top to bottom:
Gooseneck loosestrife
Primrose
Cowslip

Rose family, *Rosaceae*

This family contains a great many plants of huge culinary or ornamental value: for example, apples, pears, cherries, quince, almonds, peaches, strawberries and raspberries. Almost all require pollination, and most have simple, dish-like flowers with creamy-white petals that are visited by a broad range of short-tongued bees and hoverflies.

Blackberry**** *Rubus fruticosus,* bramble

I spend a considerable portion of my time in the garden hacking back and digging up brambles, which sprout, triffid-like, from hedges and shrubberies. I'm not trying to get rid of them: just stop them taking over. Brambles are a ubiquitous native plant, a total thug in the garden, and not especially beautiful, but there is no getting away from the fact that they are a great favourite with insects. In July and August brambles are the primary nectar supply for insects living in the countryside. Additionally the fruits are delicious, making fabulous jam or wine, and if you don't eat them the birds will. Thornless cultivated varieties are available, and are worth growing for the larger fruit. If you do wish to propagate blackberries, they will take from cuttings of all types, while any stem that touches the ground will quickly take root.

Meadowsweet   *Raspberry*

Meadowsweet**, *Filipendula ulmaria*

A common perennial wild flower found in damp meadows, marshes and ditch-banks, meadowsweet grows to about 1 m tall and produces frothy sprays of numerous tiny cream flowers from June to August. The flowers produce little nectar, but the pollen seems to be very popular with bumblebees; in Scotland this is one of the most common pollen types collected by buff-tailed bumblebees. Meadowsweet is useful for damp and lightly shaded areas. It is easily propagated by dividing clumps in early spring.

Raspberry***, *Rubus idaeus*

Raspberry is a native plant in the UK, although it is much more familiar as a plant grown in the soft fruit patch. The white, dangling flowers are inconspicuous, but nonetheless exceedingly popular with some bumblebee species, particularly early bumblebees and tree bumblebees. Of course, the fruits are also delicious. Where they are grown on a commercial scale, which is mainly in Scotland in the UK, commercial colonies of buff-tailed bumblebees are often purchased to ensure pollination.

Raspberries are best bought as canes in winter, which slowly spread and can be divided as required. I particularly like the autumn fruiting varieties, which fruit on new growth and can simply be cut to the ground in winter, rather than summer varieties, which fruit on last year's growth and so need the canes tying in over winter.

St John's Wort family, *Hypericaceae*

A large family of herbs and shrubs, many of which are used in herbal medicine, particularly for the treatment of depression.

St John's Wort**, *Hypericum perforatum*

This is a fairly common, native perennial plant of meadows and weedy places. It forms spreading clumps, with flower spikes up to about 1 m tall bearing the unusual yellow flowers, which sport clusters of very long yellow stamens, giving them a fluffy appearance. Flowering continues from June to August. White-tailed and buff-tailed bumblebees in particular will enthusiastically collect the pollen. There are also larger, shrubby species of St John's wort that are available from garden centres and are similarly attractive to bees. St John's wort will grow almost anywhere apart from complete shade or heavily waterlogged ground, and is easy to propagate from seeds, by dividing clumps, or from softwood cuttings.

Stonecrop family, *Crassulaceae*

An unusual plant family, comprising many succulent species with small, fleshy leaves, well adapted to living in arid or cold places where water is in short supply. Several species are commonly grown in rockeries, and some are now widely used on green roofs.

Ice plant****, *Hylotelephium spectabile*

This striking plant flowers in late summer through autumn, providing plate-sized arrays of tiny pink flowers that are famously attractive to butterflies fattening up for their winter hibernation. Some varieties of this species attract no insects at all, I suspect because they have no nectar. 'Autumn Joy', on the other hand, is excellent, attracting not just butterflies but also plenty of bees and hoverflies. Ice plants are highly drought-resistant, but they do need a sunny position. Being fairly short plants, they are perhaps best grown at the front of a border, or in a rockery. Sedums take very easily from softwood or semi-ripe cuttings.

Umbellifer family, *Apiaceae*

Umbellifers are easily recognised by their large 'inflorescences': umbrella-shaped arrangements of many hundreds of tiny flowers, usually white or yellow. Hogweed and cow parsley are very familiar wild umbellifers. Umbellifers are generally not so popular with larger bees such as bumblebees, as each tiny flower has only a very small portion of nectar, but they are great for a host of smaller, solitary bees, wasps, hoverflies and beetles. The wild hogweed in my garden is alive with insects in July, though it seeds everywhere and is quite invasive. If you have a meadow area, grow wild carrot: the lacy white flowers are quite beautiful, and a staple for a diversity of pollinators. Alternatively, just leave the carrots and parsnips in your veggie patch in the ground and let them flower the following year. If you haven't got a veggie patch, simply plant a carrot or parsnip, or both, in early spring, and see what happens.

Angelica***, *Angelica archangelica, Angelica gigas*

Angelica is a great favourite with wasps, hoverflies, beetles, and many of the smaller solitary bees. The large clusters of tiny white flowers provide a banquet for short-tongued pollinators to browse upon. *A. archangelica* is the most commonly grown species, and reaches about 2.5 m tall, so is definitely a plant for the back of the border. *Angelica gigas* is a dramatic, purple-leaved relative, and grows even larger. Both species prefer a deep, rich soil, and will grow in sun or partial shade. They can be grown from seed in a cold frame but, since the seedlings quickly develop a taproot, they must be pricked out when small.

*Eryngium*****, sea holly

Eryngium comprises a group of spiny, tough, thistle-like annuals and perennials found all over the world. One species, *Eryngium maritimum*, is native to the UK, and is a scarce plant found on sand dunes. Many species and varieties are cultivated, the majority of them clump-forming perennials between 30 and 80 cm in height. They prefer a sunny, well-drained position and are tolerant of both drought and poor soil. *Eryngium* bears clusters of spiky blue flowers in late summer that are attractive to bumblebees and many solitary bee species. *Eryngium planum* 'Blaukappe' seems to be one of the more attractive varieties for bees, though most are good. *Eryngium* can be reared from seed or by dividing clumps.

Lovage***, *Levisticum officinale*

I would probably never have chosen to grow lovage, but I inherited a plant when I bought my current house and garden in Sussex. Lovage is said to have many culinary uses, the leaves being a popular addition to soups in many countries, but I have tried this and found the resulting broth to be quite revolting. However, the splendid 3-metre-tall flower spikes are very attractive to soldier beetles, wasps, hoverflies and solitary bees. The soldier beetles in particular sit about in copulating pairs, mating and feeding at the same time. They then wander off to consume aphids in my vegetable patch, so I'm very happy to give the lovage garden space, despite its culinary limitations. It is best grown from seed sown in late spring.

St John's wort   *Ice plant*

Wild carrot   *Angelica*

Eryngium   *Lovage*

Vervain family, *Verbenaceae*

*Verbena bonariensis***

This is a short-lived perennial plant from South America that produces exceptionally tall, slender flower stems up to 2 m, with clusters
of small purple flowers from July through to November. The flowers
are particularly attractive to butterflies and hummingbird hawk
moths, because they hide their nectar in deep tubes where only long-
tongued insects like these can reach it. *Verbena bonariensis* thrives in
a sunny position on almost any soil. Although a tall plant, it casts
little shade and works well when grown with other, shorter plants
such as catmint in a herbaceous border. It tends to self-seed freely
but, if you need to actively propagate it, the easiest way is via softwood cuttings.

Willowherb family, *Onagraceae*

Some willowherbs can be annoying weeds – springing up, flowering and setting seed seemingly before one can blink. Nonetheless, this family includes some beautiful wild flowers, some of which are much favoured by bees.

Evening primrose*, *Oenothera biennis* and *Oenothera glazioviana*

Tall, elegant biennial plants (up to 1.5 m high) originating in North America, but now often found naturalised in the UK. The delicate, floppy, yellow flowers open so fast in the evening that you can actually watch the petals unfurling. The flowers are very short-lived, withering at midday the following day, but new ones are produced continually, and evening primrose can flower from June to September. Although evening primrose is probably pollinated mainly by moths, it is also visited in the morning by a range of bee species in search of pollen. The oil-rich seeds are a good food source for birds such as goldfinch, too. The stems, leaves, roots, flower buds and seeds are all edible for humans, making this a very versatile plant. Evening primrose prefers a sunny, well-drained site, and grows easily and rapidly from seed. Sow in early summer for flowering the following year.

Fuchsia**, *Fuchsia magellanica*

Handsome South American plants which can become sizeable shrubs in the very mildest parts of the UK. The attractive pink or white pendent flowers are pollinated by hummingbirds and the giant golden bumblebee, *Bombus dahlbomii*, in their native range. In the UK they are a popular nectar source for our longer-tongued bumblebees. Fuchsia have a long flowering period, from early summer through the autumn. They also produce edible but odd-tasting purple berries.

Fuchsias generally prefer light shade, and are readily propagated from cuttings at any time in the growing season.

Rosebay willowherb***, *Chamerion angustifolium*

A very impressive native perennial wildflower, bearing spires of pink flowers up to 2.5 m tall from July to September. The nectar-rich flowers are highly attractive to honey bees, and also attract buff-tailed and common carder bumblebees and various solitary bees. They will also collect the pollen, which is an odd blueish-green colour. Famously, rosebay willowherb became very common in London during and after the Second Wold War, invading the rubble left behind by the Blitz. This species also often invades quickly after fires or woodland clearance, but then tends to disappear as other plant species replace it. Although a very handsome plant and great for bees, in the garden rosebay willowherb can become a problematic weed, spreading by both the wind-borne seeds and underground rhizomes, and so is probably not a good choice for a herbaceous border. It is best confined to wild areas. If you do wish to propagate it, taking sections of rhizome is the easiest method.

Right, top: Evening primrose, middle: Fuchsia, bottom: Rosebay willowherb

CHAPTER EIGHT

Trees and Shrubs for Bees

When we wonder how best to provide food for pollinators, it would be pretty herbaceous plants such as lavender or catmint most of us would think of first. However, the simple height of flowering shrubs and trees means they can provide an abundance of flowers that far exceeds that of any herbaceous plant – just look up at a horse chestnut tree in full flower and you will see countless thousands of flowers and many hundreds of bees. Of course, you may not have room for full-sized trees, but many smaller shrubs and dwarf versions of large tree species are available that are suitable for almost any size of garden, and by going upwards you can pack more flowers into your space, whatever its size.

Many of the shrubs and trees mentioned here have a further value, in that they produce valuable fruit for human consumption or for birds and mammals. These fruits can be vital to the survival of some wildlife species in the winter months when food is generally in short supply. What is more, woody shrubs and trees provide nest sites for birds, crannies for insects to hibernate, and places for spiders to build their webs. If they are native species, they may also provide food for a broad range of herbivorous insects, from the caterpillars of butterflies and moths to the grubs of gall wasps. Plus, of course, if you grow a tree you are locking up carbon in the trunk, carbon that will hopefully be trapped there for decades, maybe even hundreds of years. It is a small contribution to battling climate change, but every little helps.

Apple***, *Malus pumila* (family Rosaceae)

Most of us grow apples primarily for the fruit, but they are a good source of forage for bumblebee queens in April and May, for red mason bees, which are mainly active at this time of year, and also for some mining bees that emerge early in spring. Of course, the bee visits help to ensure a good crop. All varieties of apple seem to be pretty good, but some of the crab apples, such as 'John Downie', produce particularly profuse flowers and are also very attractive to the human eye. The small, sharp fruits hang attractively into winter until consumed by birds. The fruits also give zing to cider or apple wine, and are commonly used for jelly. Tiny apple trees on dwarfing root-stocks are available for small gardens. The cheapest way to get hold of apple trees and other fruit trees is by buying them bare-rooted in the winter months; there are several excellent online nurseries (see 'Useful Addresses')

Blackthorn**, *Prunus spinosa* (family *Rosaceae*)

Blackthorn is a very common, spiny, hedgerow shrub, which is often cut back too vigorously so that it fails to flower. If you have some in a hedge, leave sections uncut each year and you will be rewarded with an abundance of snowy white flowers in March, before the leaves appear. The flowers are visited by bumblebee queens and some of the early-emerging mining bees such as the tawny mining bee (*Andrena fulva*) and orange-tailed mining bee (*Andrena haemorrhoa*). Later in the year you will be further rewarded by a crop of sloes, which make excellent wine or sloe gin.

Blackthorn can be grown fairly readily from softwood cuttings taken in June.

Above: Apple, below: Blackthorn

189

Butterfly bush or buddleia***,
Buddleja davidii (family *Scrophulariaceae*)

Buddleia is a fast-growing shrub up to 3 m tall, producing long, tapering flower heads in purple, mauve or white in summer. It is famous as a popular nectar source for butterflies, but is enjoyed too by bumblebees and moths. I often see young queen buff-tailed bumblebees on this, fattening up before going into hibernation in July/August. If you have room for several buddleia bushes, cut them back hard at different times, either after flowering in September or in April; that way you get staggered flowering for more of the summer.

Buddleia is originally from China, and is loathed by some as an invasive weed, a problem that seems to be particularly acute along railway cuttings and embankments, but I'm not convinced that growing one in your garden can make this problem any worse. Buddleia takes very easily from cuttings and, once you have one, seedlings will inevitably pop up elsewhere.

A related species, the orange-ball tree, *Buddleja globosa,* is also worth considering. It is less attractive to butterflies but more popular with bees.

Ceanothus   *Cherry*

*Ceanothus***, Californian lilac (family Rhamnaceae)

Various species are available, varying from prostrate shrubs less than 1 m in height up to small trees of 6 m or so, some deciduous and others evergreen. All bear a profusion of clusters of tiny blue flowers in late spring or late summer. *Ceanothus* can be susceptible to harsh frosts, and prefers a sunny, south-facing location if possible, but is otherwise quite easy to grow and a very handsome shrub, particularly favoured by short-tongued bumblebees such as the early bumblebee. It can be propagated from softwood cuttings in late spring.

Cherry***, *Prunus avium* (family *Rosaceae*)

Cherries are lovely and versatile trees, available in a range of sizes suitable for small or large gardens, and in a range of varieties, some of which are primarily grown for the beautiful pink spring blossom, and others for the fruit. Avoid the double-flowered ornamental varieties, mutants in which the pollen-producing anthers are replaced by extra petals. All single varieties are of interest to honey bees and queen bumblebees, red mason bees, tawny mining bees and ashy mining bees. Of course, the fruits are delicious too but, unless you net them, the birds will eat them long before they are ripe.

Cotoneaster horizontalis*** (family *Rosaceae*)

A perennial low-growing shrub that makes excellent ground cover, is very undemanding, and will be abuzz with bee activity in early summer when it produces its small pink or white flowers. It is particularly favoured by short-tongued species such as the early bumblebee and the tree bumblebee. The bright red berries of cotoneaster also provide a valuable winter food source for birds. As with buddleia, cotoneaster can be invasive in the wild, notably on chalk grassland. Many other species of cotoneaster are available, some of them growing into small trees, and most of them are attractive to bees. Propagation is easiest by taking semi-ripe cuttings in July or August.

Elaeagnus x submacrophylla***, oleaster, Russian olive, silverberry (family *Elaeagnaceae*)

A tough evergreen shrub up to 4 m tall, making an attractive stand-alone plant or suitable for use as a hedge. The leaves are a glossy dark green on top, but have silvery undersides. Clusters of small, highly scented, creamy-white flowers are borne in autumn, and can attract large numbers of honey bees and queen bumblebees fattening up for hibernation. *Elaeagnus* are versatile plants: aside from feeding bees, they are drought- and wind-tolerant, so good for exposed and coastal situations. They fix nitrogen in their roots, so if you prune the plant and use its leaves as mulch or compost you are adding nitrogen to your garden. Finally, they produce pleasantly edible fruits in April, a time when no other garden-grown fruits are available. *Elaeagnus* are best propagated using semi-hardwood cuttings or hardwood cuttings in late summer or autumn.

Cotoneaster

Elaeagnus

Escallonia*** (family *Escalloniaceae*)

This is a very hardy evergreen shrub growing up to about 3 m tall, suitable for hedging and often used as a windbreak in coastal areas. It bears numerous small pink or cream-coloured flowers in summer which are very attractive to short-tongued bumblebees. *Escallonia* can be propagated from cuttings at almost any time of the year.

*Euphorbia mellifera***** (family *Euphorbiaceae*)

This is a handsome evergreen shrub growing to about 2 m tall and originating from Madeira and the Canary Islands. It is sometimes known as honey spurge, due to the strong scent of honey the small orange and yellow flowers produce. The flowers, which appear in June and July, are very attractive to honey bees and to various solitary bees and hoverflies. The closely related *Euphorbia stygiana* is also worth considering. It is found only on the Azores, where it is an endangered species in the wild, but it can be obtained from specialist nurseries in the UK. I have seen it covered in ashy mining bees (*A. cinerea*) at Kew Gardens. Hybrids between the two species are also available, known as *Euphorbia* × *pasteurii*. All of them require full sun and a well-drained soil. They are highly resistant to drought. These *Euphorbias* can be propagated by dividing clumps or from basal cuttings.

False acacia**, *Robinia pseudoacacia* (family *Fabaceae*)

False acacia, or black locust as it is known in its native North America, is a substantial tree growing to 25 m in height, and bearing abundant cream-coloured, pea-like flowers in June. The flowers have a lovely scent and are a favoured nectar source for honey bees and bumblebees. False acacia does not flower well in the north of the UK, and prefers a sandy soil. It produces numerous suckers, and can become invasive in the countryside. Removing suckers from an existing tree is probably the easiest means of propagation, though it will also sprout from root cuttings.

Top: (l) Escallonia (r) Euphorbia mellifera
Middle: (l) False acacia (r) Firethorn
Bottom: (l) Flowering currant (r) Hawthorn

Firethorn**, *Pyracantha coccinea* (family *Rosaceae*)

Firethorn is an attractive evergreen shrub which is often grown against walls or as a hedge, reaching about 4 m in height. It produces an abundance of small frothy white blooms in May and June that are highly attractive to pollinators, particularly mining bees. These are followed by clusters of attractive bright red or orange berries in autumn, which are much loved by blackbirds and thrushes. Firethorn is fairly easy to cultivate from cuttings in summer.

Flowering currant****, *Ribes sanguineum* (family *Grossulariaceae*)

Flowering currants are shrubs growing up to about 2 m tall, closely related to blackcurrants, redcurrants, gooseberries etc. They flower in early spring from late March onwards, coming into flower just as the pussy willow is ending. I see many bumblebee queens on mine, both those that have recently emerged from hibernation and some that are already collecting pollen for their young brood. Flowering currants have very pretty tresses of pink or white flowers, while the flowers of the fruiting varieties are tiny and drab, but all are visited by bumblebees. In my garden the redcurrants are also visited every spring by the beautiful tawny mining bee, *Andrena fulva*. Currants thrive in sun or partial shade, and propagate well via layering or from semi-ripe cuttings.

Hawthorn**, *Crataegus monogyna* (family *Rosaceae*)

Hawthorn is the most common plant used in hedgerows, its sharp spines and tangled branches making excellent barriers to livestock. If not flailed too hard, or when grown as a free-standing tree, which can reach up to 8 m tall, hawthorns produce a mass of scented white blossom in May, attractive to bumblebees, honey bees and solitary bees such as mining and sweat bees. Honey from hawthorn is regarded as very high quality. The flowers are followed by the small red haws, which are an important food source for birds in winter. Pink-flowered ornamental varieties of hawthorn are available, including 'double' varieties useless for insect life. Hawthorn can be propagated from seed or via hardwood cuttings.

Heathers***, *Erica carnea* and others (family *Ericaceae*)

A great many species and varieties of heather are available. Our native species flower in summer and autumn, but for garden bees perhaps the most useful is *Erica carnea*, a species from southern Europe that flowers in late winter and early spring, a time when queen bumble-bees are recovering from hibernation and in urgent need of food. Heathers are compact, spreading evergreen bushes, usually no more than 80 cm tall, with clusters of purple, pink or white flowers. They tend to prefer acid soils, but *Erica carnea* does fine in most soils so long as it has plenty of organic matter. In the wild, heathers form extensive stands in areas of Britain with acidic soils, particularly the peaty soils of upland Britain, and here they are the staple food of some of our rarer bumblebees, such as the heath bumblebee (*B. jonellus*), bilberry bumblebee (*B. monticola)* and the northern white-tailed bumblebee (*B. magnus*). I find heathers are not easy to propagate, but it can be done by taking semi-ripe cuttings. The pot containing the cuttings is best sealed in a clear plastic bag and placed in a shady place; rooting can take several months.

Horse chestnut****, *Aesculus hippocastanum* (family *Sapindaceae*)

Native to southern Europe, horse chestnuts are commonly planted as specimen trees in the UK. They grow to 30 metres or more, so are only suitable for a large garden. However, if you do have room for one they are beautiful trees, producing frothy masses of white flowers in late April and May which provide plentiful reddish-brown pollen and abundant nectar, attracting honey bees and bumblebees. The seeds are the familiar 'conkers', and germinate readily enough, but you need to be patient, as it will be many years before a conker turns into a tree that is large enough to flower. As the old Greek proverb says, 'A society grows great when old men plant trees whose shade they know they shall never sit in.'

Laburnum****, *Laburnum x watereri* (family *Fabaceae*)

A small but handsome deciduous tree reaching up to about 8 m and originating in southern Europe, the laburnum produces glorious cascades of hanging yellow, pea-type flowers in May and June. Laburnums prefer a sunny position, and make lovely specimen plants for the centre of a lawn, or sometimes they are trained to create archways. The flowers are mainly visited by bumblebees, particularly red-tails, which have a strong preference for yellow. Laburnums are very slow to root from cuttings, but can be grown from seeds, which should be sown in autumn and left outside during the winter, after which they will usually germinate. Note that all parts of laburnum, and particularly the seeds, are poisonous.

Lime****, *Tilia spp.* (family *Malvaceae*, mallows)

Eventually becoming huge and beautiful trees (more than 40 metres tall), limes should only be considered for planting if you have a lot of space and patience. There are a number of closely related and easily confused species, the most common being the native small-leaved lime (*Tilia cordata*), the large-leaved lime (*Tilia platyphyllos*) from continental Europe, and hybrids of the two, often known as common lime (*Tilia x europaea*). All produce inconspicuous but highly fragrant, greenish flowers in June and July, which are hugely attractive to honey bees and short-tongued bumblebees, particularly buff-, white- and red-tailed bumblebees. A lime tree in full flower will hum with the activity of literally thousands of bees, particularly in the morning when most of the nectar is produced. Honey bees produce a distinctive and very pleasant honey from limes.

Lime trees are very frequently infested with aphids, and their leaves can become sticky with honeydew (a sugary excretion produced by aphids). Both honey bees and bumblebees can sometimes be seen collecting this too, though the honey made from this aphid poo is said to be less appealing.

Dead bees are very often found beneath lime trees, particularly silver lime (*Tilia tomentosa*) and also sometimes common lime. Bumblebees seem to be worst affected, though occasionally honey bees are seen too, and sometimes dozens of bodies are present. Despite considerable discussion and some investigation, no completely satisfying explanation has ever been put forward. My best guess is that the bodies simply reflect the vast numbers of bees visiting the trees – bees have to die some time, the workers typically only lasting a few weeks, and if thousands of them are visiting a tree then one might expect a portion of them to expire while doing so.

Do not confuse these limes with the citrus tree of the same name, which is entirely unrelated.

Mahonia species***, Oregon grape (family *Berberidaceae*)

A woody evergreen shrub growing to about 4 m tall, *Mahonia* flowers in December and January, producing sprays of small, bright-yellow flowers which are one of the main food sources at this time of year for winter-active buff-tailed bumblebees. The purple, tangy berries in spring are a tasty snack for us humans, or a welcome treat for blackbirds and thrushes. *Mahonia* is a useful shrub, as it is one of few that will thrive in shade. It can be propagated from semi-ripe cuttings or via seed, though the latter require exposure to frost or a month in the fridge before they will germinate.

*Top: (l) Heather
(r) Horse chestnut*

*Middle: (l) Laburnum
(r) Lime*

Bottom: Mahonia

199

Medlar**, *Mespilus germanica* (family *Rosaceae*)

Medlars were once prized for their unusual edible fruits, but fell out of favour in the twentieth century and are now little grown. This is a shame, as they are beautiful small trees up to about 6 m with charmingly twisted branches and an abundance of large white blossoms in May. They are visited for nectar by a range of bumblebees, honey bees and mining bees. Medlars are usually bought grafted on to rootstocks which determine their eventual size.

Pear*, *Pyrus communis* (family *Rosaceae*)

Pears produce a beautiful show of creamy blossom in April, usually just before most apple varieties are in bloom. The nectar tends to be a little less sweet than that of apples, so many visitors to pear blossom tend to be collecting the pollen. Pears are pollinated by a broad range of bees, including honey bees, bumblebees, both the ashy and tawny mining bees and red mason bees. Pear varieties are said to vary greatly in their attractiveness to pollinators, but I am aware of no attempts to work out which are most attractive. In my garden 'Concorde' seems to be among the most attractive varieties, and produces a reliable crop of dessert pears too. As with most other fruit trees, the rootstock determines the size of the tree. If grown on wild pear rootstock (*Pyrus communis*), pears can grow into very splendid, columnar trees to 10 m or more, although you might have to wait ten years to get any blossom or fruit.

Plum**, *Prunus domestica* (family *Rosaceae*)

There are hundreds of varieties of plum and damson, although only a dozen or so are widely available. The snow-white blossom is produced in abundance from late March through to early May, depending on the variety, and is attractive to short-tongued bumblebee queens, honey bees and various early solitary bees. In my garden the orange-tailed mining bee (*Andrena haemmorrhoa*) is very abundant on plum blossom, the males scouting the flowers for feeding females. The ripe fruits are, of course, delicious to eat, but leave a few juicy ones to ferment on the ground and you will also provide a feast for wasps and butterflies.

Pussy willow*****, *Salix caprea* (family *Salicaceae*)

Pussy willow is worth a special mention, as the yellow catkins are one of the best pollen and nectar sources for queen bumblebees in early spring when very little else is available. There are also a number of early solitary bees, particularly mining bees, that are heavily dependent on willow. This is a native tree species, growing to 10 m or more. Luckily dwarf, prostrate and weeping ornamental varieties are available that take up far less space. The trees are either male (producing pollen and a bit of nectar) or female (producing nectar), so one of each is ideal if you have room, but, if you can only fit in one, go for a male (they are also prettier). Pussy willow will grow almost anywhere, and takes very easily from cuttings; stems simply pushed into the ground will often take root.

*Rhododendron**** (family *Ericaceae*)

Rhododendrons are woody shrubs, both evergreen and deciduous, originating primarily from Asia and North America. They vary in size from tiny alpine shrubs to sizeable trees of 15 m or more. Numerous species, hybrids and varieties of *Rhododendron* are available, all having beautiful, showy spring blossoms in purple, pink, red, yellow or white. Double varieties are available, but best avoided. *Rhododendron ponticum,* a native of Iberia and Turkey, has become an important invasive weed, particularly in western Britain, and so it is now illegal to plant it. The nectar of *Rhododendron* contains low concentrations of a poison known as grayanotoxin, which can be lethal to honey bees, but seems to have much less or no effect on bumblebees.

As a result, honey bees seem to avoid it, but long- and short-tongued bumblebees are highly attracted, collecting both nectar and pollen.

Rhododendrons prefer an acid soil, although they seem able to grow pretty well in neutral soils. Otherwise, they are very versatile plants, able to grow in sun or shade, and providing excellent ground cover if you are after a low-maintenance garden. Rhododendrons are not easy to propagate; but can be grown from seeds sown on the surface of compost, though germination is very slow. Layering is effective but also slow, while cuttings in late autumn sometimes take.

Rose***, *Rosa* species (family *Rosaceae*)

Roses are among the most familiar of ornamental plants, having been cultivated for millennia. There are over 300 species and countless cultivars, all of them woody shrubs or climbers, mainly originating in Europe and Asia. The native *Rosa canina* is a common plant of hedgerows and scrubby places, bearing attractive pink and cream flowers in May and June. Most roses have large, attractive blossoms in pink, red, yellow or white, and some modern varieties have very long flowering periods. Sadly, a great many of the rose varieties on sale are double varieties, which are useless to pollinators. The single varieties – ones in which the yellow pollen-covered stamens are readily visible – are very attractive to bees. Bumblebees and some solitary bees have mastered the art of buzz pollination, in which they emit audible bursts of high-frequency vibrations by buzzing their flight muscles. They do this while dashing around the centre of the rose, the vibrations shaking free pollen, which they gather up with their hairy legs.

Roses provide the added value of producing edible and pretty red hips in autumn. These make a nice jam or jelly, and are also much appreciated by birds over the winter. Roses are best propagated from cuttings in late summer or autumn. They do suffer from aphids and various other pests, but please don't be tempted to spray your roses with insecticides. Do nothing, and the worst that can happen is that your rose will look a bit peaky and produce fewer blossoms.

Medlar

Pear

Plum

Pussy willow

Rhododendron

Rose

Scotch Broom   *Sycamore*

Scotch Broom**, *Cytisus scoparius* (family *Fabaceae*, peas)

A familiar wild shrub growing to about 2 m, and covered in yellow flowers in late spring. In the UK broom is largely dependent on bumblebees for pollination, for most other insects are not large enough to 'trigger' the flowers, which requires the insect to push down the 'keel' of the flower to expose the pollen-covered anthers. Interestingly, broom is regarded as a noxious weed in New Zealand, Australia and North America, where it is not native. In the UK it makes a very attractive garden shrub, preferring reasonably well-drained soils and a sunny situation. Scotch broom is fairly easy to grow from seed, and also takes from semi-ripe cuttings in late summer.

Sycamore**, *Acer pseudoplatanus* and relatives (family *Sapindaceae*)

Sycamores were introduced to the UK in the Middle Ages, and are now one of our commonest large trees. They are not widely rec-ognised as bee plants, for their flowers are small, green, and easily overlooked. No-one, though, has told the bees, which enthusiastic-ally gather nectar and pollen from them in April and May. In my garden, common carder bumblebees seem particularly attracted to sycamore, but it also attracts honey bees and solitary bees such as the tawny mining bee. Our native field maple (*Acer campestre*) is simi-larly attractive to bees, but is a much smaller and more manageable tree and useful for hedging.

Tree mallow***, *Lavatera x clementii* (family *Malvaceae*, mallows)

A short-lived, woody shrub related to hollyhocks, tree mallow is extremely easy to grow, and produces masses of very attractive hollyhock-type pink flowers through the summer from June onwards. It produces plentiful pollen and nectar, attracting both honey bees and a range of short-tongued bumblebees. Tree mallow takes very readily from cuttings, and rapidly grows to about 2 m tall, although it then often flops over in an untidy heap. It is wise to replace plants every few years with new ones, as older plants can die off in wet winters.

Wayfaring Tree***, *Viburnum lantana (family Caprifoliaceae)*

A small native tree or large shrub, growing to about 4 m tall and producing clusters of small white flowers in May. Bees, butterflies and hoverflies visit the flowers, while blackbirds, fieldfares and waxwings (if you are very lucky) eat the red berries in autumn and winter. Dormice and wood mice are also said to enjoy the fruits, though they are mildly poisonous to humans. Wayfaring trees are not fussy about soil type, will grow in sun or partial shade, and can be grown as small specimen trees of used in hedging. They take easily from softwood or semi-ripe cuttings.

Tree mallow

Wayfaring tree

CHAPTER NINE

Flowers for Pollinators Through the Year

Bees and their young eat only nectar and pollen, and so are entirely dependent on an adequate supply of the right kinds of flowers throughout their flight season. If you would like to provide the perfect environment for bees in your garden, therefore, it's important to try to ensure there are suitable plants flowering from late February to October. The added benefit is that there is always colour and life in your garden. In an ideal world, your flower selection would also cater for the full range of different pollinating insects, including both short- and long-tongued bumblebees, and also solitary bees, hover-flies, butterflies, moths, beetles, parasitic wasps and honey bees, so that each of the pollinator species has food at the appropriate time in their life cycle. All of them have slightly different (but often over-lapping) flower preferences, depending on their shape, size, tongue length and so on. Of course, in reality, unless you have an estate the size of Kew Gardens and an awful lot of time on your hands, it is impossible to cater for all possible pollinators all of the time. Don't fret or be downhearted: if there is a gap in your provision, hopefully the insects will be able to buzz over the garden fence and find some-thing to keep them going in one of your neighbours' gardens. Rest assured that any flowers you provide are a bonus for the insects and, if you simply grow as many of the right kinds of plants as you can, then you will be doing them a huge service.

Try to squeeze in at least one or two plants from each of the time periods listed below. Some have very long flowering seasons, and so occur in multiple boxes. I have crudely divided plants into those visited by short-tongued pollinators (many bumblebees, almost all solitary bees, hoverflies, wasps and beetles) and those visited by long-tongued pollinators (some bumblebees, moths and butterflies). The ones in bold are suggestions for the very best plants: ones with long flowering periods and which attract diverse insects.

Flowering time	Short-tongues	Long-tongues
February to April	Blackthorn	Bluebell
	Crocus	Ground Ivy
	Dandelion	**Lungwort**
	Grape hyacinth	Primrose
	Heather (*Erica carnea*)	Red dead-nettle
	Hellebore	Rosemary
	Flowering Currant	White dead-nettle
	Pear	
	Plum	
	Pussy willow	
May & June	Apple	Green alkanet
	Bistort	*Aquilegia*
	Broom	Bugle
	Bugle	Bush vetch
	Campanula	**Comfrey**
	Ceanothus	Cowslip
	Cherry	*Dicentra*
	Chives	Foxglove
	Comfrey	Honeywort
	Cotoneaster	Iris
	Erysimum	Kidney vetch
	False acacia	Meadow vetchling
	Firethorn	Red campion
	Geranium	*Rhododendron*

Flowering time	Short-tongues	Long-tongues
	Hawthorn	*Salvia*
	Horse chestnut	Selfheal
	Jacob's ladder	Yellow rattle
	Kidney Vetch	
	Laburnum	
	Lime	
	Meadow rue	
	Medlar	
	Ox-eye daisy	
	Raspberry	
	Rhododendron	
	Rose	
	Salvia	
	Speedwell	
	Thrift	
	Wayfaring tree	
	Wisteria	
July & August	*Allium*	*Allium*
	Angelica	Black horehound
	Bird's-foot trefoil	Buddleia
	Borage	Burdock
	Bramble	Bush vetch
	Californian poppy	**Catmint**
	Caryopteris	*Centaurea*
	Cardoon	Everlasting pea
	Catmint	Figwort
	Centaurea	*Fuchsia*
	Cosmos	Hedge woundwort
	Culver's root	Hemp agrimony
	Dahlia	Honeysuckle
	Eryngium	Lamb's ear
	Escallonia	Marsh skullcap
	Euphorbia mellifera	*Monarda*
	Evening primrose	Nasturtium

Flowering time	Short-tongues	Long-tongues
July & August contd.	**Field scabious**	*Penstemon*
	Figwort	***Phacelia***
	Giant hyssop	*Phlomis*
	Globe thistle	Plume thistle
	Heathers	Purple toadflax
	(summer flowering)	Red clover
	Helenium	Red valerian
	Hemp agrimony	Runner beans
	Hollyhock	Sainfoin
	Hydrangea petiolaris	*Salvia*
	Hydrangea serratifolia	Snapdragon
	Hyssop	Teasel
	Lavender	Tufted vetch
	Leek	*Verbena bonariensis*
	Lovage	**Viper's bugloss**
	Love-in-a-mist	
	Lupin	
	Marigold	
	Marjoram	
	Meadowsweet	
	Mint	
	Mullein	
	Musk mallow	
	Phacelia	
	Poppy	
	Ragwort	
	Raspberry	
	Rose	
	Rosebay willowherb	
	Salvia	
	St John's wort	
	Sunflower	
	Thyme	
	Tree mallow	
	Viper's bugloss	

Flowering time	Short-tongues	Long-tongues
	Wild carrot	
	White bryony	
	White clover	
	Wood sage	
September	*Chrysanthemum*	**Devil's bit scabious**
to October	*Dahlia*	*Fuchsia*
	Devil's bit scabious	Ice plant
	Eleagnus	*Nasturtium*
	Goldenrod	
	Helenium	
	Ice plant	
	Ivy	
	Michaelmas daisy	
	Passion flower	

Propagation Techniques

In the sections on plants, shrubs and trees above, a number of propagation techniques are mentioned which may not all be familiar to the novice gardener. Here they are explained. Propagating plants can be very rewarding, is usually quite easy, and can save you an absolute fortune that might otherwise be spent buying plants from your local garden centre. It is also much more environmentally friendly: plants you buy will usually have been treated with many pesticides, are often grown in peat-based composts and sold in disposable plastic pots and may well have been shipped hundreds of miles from where they were mass-reared, often in continental Europe. Growing your own avoids all of this, enabling you to produce truly 'green' plants.

From seed

If you are an experienced gardener you might assume that everybody surely knows how to grow plants from seed, but a surprising number of people have no idea how. It strikes me as a basic life skill that ought to be taught in schools. Fortunately, it is easy to learn and usually very simple and rewarding, an almost magical process of green life bursting from a tiny dried seed. The basic idea is very simple. If seeds are exposed to water and oxygen (some also need light), they will usually germinate, sending a root downwards and tender young leaves up to the light. Some seeds, such as those of most cabbage family plants, germinate within just a few days. Others require more patience, and with a few you may have to wait months before anything happens.

The optimum timing of sowing depends on the plant, and purchased seeds will always give advice on the packet. For seeds you have collected yourself, sowing them in March on a windowsill indoors or from April onwards outside will usually work. Some seeds require vernalisation, a period of cold, before they will germinate, an adaptation that in nature ensures they germinate in spring. Such seeds can be sown in September and left outside, or in an unheated greenhouse through the winter.

For all but the largest seeds, it is usual to sow them in seed trays. Big seeds such as beans or pumpkins are more usually sown individually in pots. Runner beans I tend to sow in the cardboard centres from toilet rolls, packed into a seed tray; when ready to plant out, the whole tube can be planted into the ground, avoiding disturbing the seedling's delicate roots. For germinating seeds, most people prefer to use commercial compost (peat-free, of course!) as this contains no unwanted seeds – if you use homemade compost, unless it has reached a very high temperature during the composting process, there are likely to be many seeds in it, making it potentially difficult to distinguish the seedlings you were hoping to grow from the mass of other seedlings that appear. Alternatively, I find that the soil from molehills on my lawn has a nice structure and few unwanted seeds in it and so it is good for germination.

Whatever medium you use, fill your container, gently firm down the compost, and water well. Sow seeds thinly on the surface and sprinkle a very thin layer of more compost over them. If growing from purchased seed, advice on the ideal depth is usually given on the packet. For large seeds such as beans, push them individually into the compost to a depth of 2 cm and cover. It is not essential, but it often helps to cover the seed tray/pot with polythene or glass to maintain high humidity. Place the seed trays on a windowsill or in

a greenhouse or cold frame, or simply outside in a sheltered, sunny spot, ideally where slugs cannot easily reach them. Keep well watered and, with luck, you will soon see the seedling appear.

Once seedlings are established, and before they become too crowded in the seed tray, it is generally best to pot them up. Tease apart the young plants (known as 'pricking out'), being particularly careful to minimise damage to their roots, and plant them individually in small pots of compost. Grow them on for a few weeks so they are reasonably sturdy and rapidly increasing in size before planting them out where they are to flower. Water well both before and after planting out. If your plants have been reared on a windowsill or in a greenhouse, it is important to harden them off before planting outside. For two to three weeks place the plants outside in a sheltered spot during the daytime, but bring them in at night; this gives the plants chance to adjust to the colder, windier conditions outdoors.

If you haven't got the time, space or patience for sowing seeds in trays, potting them up and so on, the more haphazard approach is to sow seeds direct into the ground outside. For some plants such as our native poppies, Californian poppies, foxgloves, nasturtiums, cornflower and *Phacelia*, this is recommended anyway over sowing in trays. Simply clear an area of other plants, rake the surface to produce a fine tilth, sprinkle on your flower seeds, rake again to cover the seeds, and firm down by gently pressing the soil down with your feet. Generally this is best done once the soil has warmed up, from April onwards until September.

Softwood cuttings

Softwood cuttings are usually taken in late spring or early summer when plants are growing fast. Using a sharp knife, cut a fresh stem of new growth, avoiding flowering stems if possible. At this point it is important to process and plant the cuttings quickly, as otherwise they dehydrate and will soon die. Trim the bottom just below a leaf node (where a leaf joins the stem), and cut the top to give a total length of about 8 cm. Remove leaves from the bottom half, and pinch out the growing tip if present. If you are so inclined, dip the lower end of the stem in hormone rooting powder: this increases the chances of the cutting becoming established, but is not essential, and some like to avoid using such chemicals. Insert the cutting into a 50:50 mix of compost and sharp sand in a pot, burying half the cutting. Water well, then enclose the pot in a plastic bag and put somewhere warm and light but out of direct sunlight. Softwood cuttings are the fastest kind to set roots, usually taking from four to eight weeks. Harden them off before planting outside. Softwood cuttings work well for a large array of herbaceous plants and woody shrubs and trees, including buddleia, *Fuchsia, Lavatera,* lavender, mint, *Penstemon* and sage.

Hardwood cuttings

These are normally taken in autumn and winter, a time of year when there aren't too many other jobs that need doing in the garden. Choose healthy shoots of the current year's growth, and cut into roughly 20 cm lengths, cutting just above a bud at the top and just below a bud at the bottom. For some plants, such as lavender, rooting is encouraged by slicing off a strip of bark down one side of the lower 2 cm of the cutting. Rooting is also often improved if you dip the lower end into hormone rooting powder. Dig a shallow trench in a sheltered spot in the garden. Sprinkle a layer of coarse sand in the bottom, and then insert the cuttings so that the bottom two-thirds are buried when the trench is refilled. Cuttings can then be left until the following autumn; only weed around them and water if there is a dry spell over the summer. With luck, by then they will have developed new roots, and be showing signs of healthy growth above ground. Plants that take well from hardwood cuttings include buddleia, cotoneaster, currants, hawthorn, honeysuckle, lavender, roses and willows.

Semi-ripe cuttings

These are taken in late summer or early autumn. Select healthy sections of the current year's growth, and remove with a sharp knife or secateurs, cutting just below a leaf node. As with softwood cuttings, it is important to process them quickly. Trim into lengths of about 12 cm, and remove the leaves from the bottom half. If there is a fresh tip of new growth, cut this off. If the leaves are large, such as in passion flowers, cut them in half by slicing across at right angles to the central vein: this reduces the surface area of leaf and thus reduces water loss. Dip the lower end in hormone rooting powder and insert into pots containing an equal mix of sharp sand and compost, down to approximately half the length of the cutting. Water well, then place the cuttings in a greenhouse, or cover with a plastic bag and place on a windowsill. If all goes well, the cuttings should be ready to pot up and harden off the following spring.

Semi-ripe cuttings work well for blackberry, *Escallonia*, flowering currants, heathers, ivy, *Mahonia*, passion flower and raspberry, among others. A variation on semi-ripe cuttings is to pull a side shoot from an older stem, in so doing ripping away a small amount of bark from the stem. The side shoot is then shortened and trimmed as above. This works better for *Ceanothus*.

Basal cuttings

Herbaceous perennial plants tend to die right back over the winter, but then send up many vigorous shoots in spring. Very often these fast-growing shoots make excellent cuttings. In late winter or early spring, use a sharp knife to cut shoots off just beneath the soil surface. Remove leaves near the bottom, and pinch out the growing point at the top. Insert the stem 2.5 cm deep into moist compost in a pot. Water well, then place a plastic bag over the pot to maintain high humidity. This approach works well for many plants such as *Helenium*, Michaelmas daisy, dead-nettles and lupins.

Root cuttings

Along with hardwood cuttings, root cuttings are normally taken in late autumn or winter, a quiet time in the garden. Root cuttings take advantage of some plants' ability to regenerate from small fragments of roots, something that is undesirable and annoying in persistent weeds like creeping thistle, but is a much more useful attribute in plants you wish to encourage.

Lift a parent plant, and cut off roots that are 1 cm thick or larger. Discard the thin end, and cut the remaining root into 5 cm-long pieces, using an angled cut at the bottom and a perpendicular cut at the top so you know which end is which. Plant vertically in a mix of compost and sharp sand, so that the top is just below the compost surface, and water well. Ideally, place the pot in an unheated greenhouse or cold frame, or just leave outside. With luck, the plant will sprout rapidly the following spring.

This method can be used to produce very large numbers of plants. For example, one large comfrey plant can produce enough root material for hundreds of root cuttings. This technique is also suitable for *Echinops, Eryngium,* Oriental poppy, passion vine, *Robinia* and *Verbascum.* It can also be used for some plants, such as *Campanula,* that have thinner roots, but in this case take a longer section, up to 12 cm in length, so the young plant has enough resources to grow. These long thin roots are best planted horizontally.

Layering

In some plants, any stem which comes into contact with the ground will take root. Brambles do this prolifically – one of the reasons they can be hard to keep in check. Layering is one of the easiest ways to obtain new plants, though you can't produce many this way as it is relatively slow. It is best done in spring, when plants are actively growing.

Select a parent plant with one or more young stems that can be bent down to the ground. Dig a shallow, 4 cm-deep trench along the line of the stem. Using a sharp knife, make an approximately 4 cm longitudinal incision in the stem, running through a leaf bud. Dusting on hormone rooting powder to the wound will help. Peg the damaged section into the trench, using a tent peg or loop of wire cut from a coat hanger. Remove any leaves that are within the trench and refill, leaving the end of the shoot protruding. The stem should send out roots, and in a year's time you can sever the connection with the parent plant and dig up the new plant.

Layering is suitable for currants, honeysuckle, ivy, *Rhododendron* and wisteria. Blackberries and loganberries can be propagated by a variation on this theme in which the tip of a shoot is buried in the ground. This will root and send up shoots.

Division

Dividing existing clumps is one of the easiest and most reliable ways of multiplying many herbaceous perennial plants. Even if you don't want lots more of them, many plants benefit from being lifted in the winter, some compost being dug in, and then healthy sections of the old plant replanted. Division of most plants is best done in the autumn or winter, but if necessary can be done at any time of year, so long as the resulting plants are given a really good watering. Irises are best divided after flowering in mid- to late summer.

Simply ease the plant out of the ground with a garden fork, and then tease apart sections of rooted shoots. Sometimes you can do this with your bare hands, but for particularly sturdy plants you might need a garden spade to slice apart the clump. The separate sections can then be planted direct into the ground or potted up to grow on before planting in their final position. A huge range of plants can be prop-agated in this way, including bugle, *Campanula,* comfrey, *Eryngium,* geranium, ice plant, Iris, Michaelmas daisy, primrose and *Salvia.*

Grafting

This is an advanced technique in which a shoot from one plant is joined to the rootstock from another. It is very widely used in fruit trees, the rootstocks being chosen primarily to control the size of the tree. Grafting is also widely used for roses. However, it is a complex technique ideally taught first-hand by an expert, and beyond the scope of this book.

CHAPTER ELEVEN

Creating Your Own Wildflower Meadow

The wild habitat most hard hit by changes to the UK countryside is flower-rich, 'unimproved' grassland such as our once extensive hay meadows and chalk downland. A hundred years ago, almost all farms were mixed, with both livestock and arable fields. At the time, one of the biggest challenges to growing arable crops was keeping the soil fertility high enough. Farmers would often 'rest' a field by leaving fallow for a year after cropping, and they incorporated legumes such as beans or clover leys into crop rotations to boost soil nitrogen. They would also apply animal manure and, in the days when most transport was by horse and cart, it made sense to rear the animals and grow crops on the same farms, so that the manure did not need to be transported far. Livestock required hay for the winter, so almost every farmer had hay meadows, areas left ungrazed through the spring to provide a hay crop in summer. Some of these hay meadows were managed in the same way for centuries, and over time they built up a glorious botanical diversity. Our farms were an interconnected patchwork of arable crops, fallow fields, clover leys, flower-rich hay meadows and grazed pasture. Our chalk hills were too infertile for arable crops, and so were grazed with sheep and cattle, creating flower-rich downlands.

At the beginning of the twentieth century cheap, synthetic fertilisers began to appear, an offshoot of the growing petrochemical industry. At the same time, motorised transport became widespread, and farming began to change. With the availability of cheap fertilisers, farmers on the best soils in the centre and east of Britain abandoned keeping livestock to grow arable crops. They no longer needed hay meadows or pasture, so these were converted to cropland. The chalk downlands, previously considered too infertile for arable cropping, were ploughed and sown with cereals, which could now be grown so long as enough of the newly available synthetic fertilisers were applied. Farmers in the wetter and less fertile west of the country could not compete at producing arable crops and came to specialise in livestock. However, in the winter they switched to feeding them on silage rather than hay. Silage is usually made from bright green swards of fast-growing rye grass, liberally sprinkled with fertiliser and cut many times a year. Once again hay meadows were swept away. The pastures where the animals grazed in summer were also treated with the new fertilisers to encourage rapid growth of grasses, and also became green, flowerless expanses. Take a train journey across Devon and you will see a rolling emerald carpet stretching to the horizon, with scarcely a flower in sight. It is hard to believe, but only 2 per cent remains of the flower-rich hay meadows and downlands we had just seventy years ago.

Sadly, this habitat was one of the best places for bumblebees. Many of the UK's rarest bee species, such as the great yellow bumblebee and the shrill carder bee, are rare precisely because they used to live in flower-rich grasslands, and their home is almost entirely gone. Their last small populations cling onto the patches of flower-rich habitat that remain: places such as Salisbury Plain and the beautiful flower-filled coastal *machair* grasslands of western Scotland.

I'm not telling you this to depress you, but in the hope of inspiring you. It is possible to re-create wildflower meadows in our gardens and parks and, perhaps if we create enough of them, these rare bees will be able to creep back into our towns and cities, along with butterflies, hoverflies, spiders, voles, beetles and much more. You may be thinking you don't have room, but even tiny mini-meadows have value for wildlife.

Before I describe the different approaches to creating your own wildlife meadow, we need a quick ecology lesson, for it's useful to understand a little about the reasons why certain flowers thrive in these ecosystems. If you visit one of our surviving patches of hay meadow or chalk downland in late spring or early summer, you will see a great diversity of different flowers: clovers, vetches, trefoils, medicks, sainfoin, knapweed, hawkbits, yellow rattle and so on. Many of them belong to the pea family, also known as legumes, because these plants have a trick which gives them an advantage over most other plants: they have root nodules packed with bacteria that are able to fix nitrogen from the air and turn it into the nitrates the plant needs to manufacture protein for growth. Put simply, they can make their own fertiliser. That is why farmers used to use legumes in crop rotations. Most soils are naturally low in nitrates, so being able to get them from the air gives legumes the edge in competition with other plants, particularly grasses, which grow very slowly in conditions of low fertility. It also means that the legumes can afford to put more protein into their pollen, which makes legume pollen an absolute favourite with bees, as it is more nutritious than that from many other plants.

Some plants use other means to gain nutrients. Yellow rattle and some other related plants such as red bartsia and eyebright are 'hemi-parasites', meaning that they are parasitic on other plants, particularly grasses. Their roots tap into the roots of nearby plants and drain them of nutrients. This is a particularly useful capability, as it reduces the vigour of the grasses, thereby leaving more room for flowers. Experimental studies have found that adding in yellow rattle can be a very useful tool for improving the biodiversity of grasslands that have few flowers.

A key attribute of both hay meadows and chalk downlands is that nutrients are in short supply. For centuries, neither habitat received much input of fertiliser, aside from an infrequent sprinkling of manure on some hay meadows, and the dung left behind by grazing animals on the downland. Counterintuitively, this low fertility led to a high abundance and diversity of flowers, because in such condition no one plant can dominate. Unfortunately, it is very easy to ruin: a few sacks of artificial fertiliser is all it takes to destroy a meadow. The grasses immediately shoot up, along with a few other thuggish, competitive plants that thrive in highly fertile conditions, such as nettle, dock and hogweed, the flowers are soon shaded out, and the bees and butterflies vanish. A consequence of all of this is that it is much easier to create your own flower-rich meadow area on land that is not very fertile. If your only option is a fertile piece of land, then reducing soil fertility is vital to prevent it quickly turning into a nettle patch, but it can be hard to do.

It is also important to understand that hay meadows and chalk downland are both man-made habitats. Without management, they rapidly get overgrown with bramble thickets and scrub, and eventually become woodland. Many believe that similar flower-rich habitats may have existed before man, maintained by the grazing action of aurochs, bison and short-tusked elephants that once roamed Europe, but these aren't entirely practical management options for a garden. If you want to create and maintain your own wildflower meadow, you'll have to be willing to cut it down at intervals, even though this might feel destructive.

Red bartsia

Meadow creation option 1:
The growbag meadow

Few of us are lucky enough to have rolling acres of garden. Some may only have access to a tiny courtyard, a small suburban garden, or perhaps just a balcony or rooftop terrace. Do not despair: you can still create something valuable and beautiful. Purchase a growbag, or fill the largest trough or other container you can fit into your space with peat-free compost, and sow with a wild-flower seed mix. Various proprietary seed mixes are available from most of the usual seed merchants and garden centres. I would recommend including any of the following: red campion, meadow clary, greater knap-weed, musk mallow, ox-eye daisy, selfheal, poppy, foxglove, bird's-foot trefoil, viper's bugloss and cornflower. Some of these are annuals, and will give colour in the first year, while others will flower the following year. Avoid seed mixes that contain meadow grasses: growbags and compost tend to have high fertility, and these will tend to take over.

Simply place your growbag or container somewhere that gets at least a little sun, sow the seeds in April or May and, as long as you remember to water regularly, you will be guaranteed a colourful display that will attract a range of insects. Bees are uncannily good at sniffing out flowers no matter where they are, even on the roof of a tower block. This is a great project for a young child who, with just a little help, can do all of this for themselves and be rewarded by seeing the seeds germinate, grow and flower, watching the insects visit, and witnessing the flowers set seed.

Meadow creation option 2:
Turning your lawn into a meadow

Most people who have a garden will have a lawn. If it was laid using lawn turf – for example, if you live on a relatively new housing estate – then it may just contain a simple mix of grasses. This may also be the case if you have recently treated your lawn with a proprietary selective weedkiller, which will take out broadleaved 'weeds' (aka flowers) and leave behind only the grass. On the other hand, most older or untreated lawns contain a diversity of interesting plants just waiting for a chance to flower. There are often clovers, both white and red, probably some dandelions and, with a bit of luck, there may also be various hawkbits, buttercups, daisies, speedwell, selfheal and perhaps some bird's-foot trefoil. Such a lawn is likely to already have low soil fertility, for regular removing of grass clippings over several years will have lowered the nutrient levels in the soil, just as happens in a hay meadow. You may well already have the makings of a wonderful meadow in your garden without realising it. All it needs is for you to relax your mowing regime.

The herbaceous plants that might be present in your lawn are all ones that can survive regular mowing, because they press themselves against the ground, creeping horizontally among the grasses. They evolved to do this to avoid being eaten by grazing herbivores, but the strategy works just as well in avoiding the blades of the mower. However, they all send up flowers on stalks so that pollinators can easily find them, and it is these that get decapitated every time you mow. Some plants like daisies can flower very quickly after being mowed, so their white and yellow flowers are a familiar sight even on close-cropped lawns. Many of the other plants are a bit slower, and so you will only see their flowers if you let the lawn grow a little.

You could reduce mowing of your whole lawn to just once a year in August, treating it like a hay meadow. You would save quite a bit of petrol or electricity and your own time, and the bees, butterflies and grasshoppers might thank you, but to most eyes this would

look shaggy and unkept for much of the year, as if you have gone on a long holiday or your house has been abandoned. When areas of public parks are deliberately left unmown to encourage wildlife there are often complaints from members of the public, who think it untidy. However, there is a solution that works well, and that is to mow neatly around the edges of the meadow area, or mow a meandering path through the middle. In public parks a clear sign saying 'Wildflower meadow' also helps, making it clear that the tall vegetation is deliberate and not the result of laziness; this makes a huge difference to public perception.

You may have only a small lawn, but even leaving a single square metre of it unmown will result in visible, tangible benefit to wildlife. Try it and, aside from flowers, you will soon see spiders busy spinning their webs, caterpillars, shield bugs and beetles – all creatures that struggle to survive in a mown lawn.

If you'd rather not leave parts of your lawn for a whole year without mowing, perhaps because you are very attached to the more formal look, then a less drastic alternative approach is to divide your lawn area in half and rotate the mowing. Instead of cutting the whole lot every two to three weeks in the growing season, as is common practice, cut half of it every three weeks, then the other half three weeks later. That way you allow time for most of the lawn plants to send up their flowers, and there is always a mown area for putting a deckchair on, or for playing games, or just for looking at.

If you are unlucky, you may have inherited a lawn which contains few flowers. Reducing cutting will result in longer grass, which will be enjoyed by some wildlife, such as spiders and voles, but it won't produce the riot of colour you might have hoped for. In this situation there are several options. A quick fix is to buy wildflower plants such as cowslips or field scabious and plant them out into your meadow area, cutting the grass short first to give them some space. A much cheaper alternative is to raise your own wildflower plants from seed in seed trays (see 'Propagation techniques'). With a little effort, one pack of seed costing a couple of pounds can produce hundreds of plants. To help the young plants establish in your meadow, you may need to hand-weed around them for a few weeks after they are planted out.

If all this hand-planting and weeding sounds like a lot of work, an alternative is to cut the grass in September or April with your mower on its lowest setting, rake the surface hard, sprinkle on a wildflower seed mix and trample it in. This is a bit hit-and-miss, and success depends on the soil fertility, the vigour of your existing grasses, and the enthusiasm of your local slug population for consuming the seedlings, but usually at least some of the flowers in the seed mix will become established. If you include some yellow rattle seed this can be particularly helpful in suppressing the grasses and encouraging flowers.

Meadow creation option 3:
The mini-meadow

If you have a square metre or two of ground (the bigger the better, but anything will do), then consider turning it into a mini-meadow. If you have no money, simply dig over the patch in autumn or spring, removing as many roots of pernicious weeds as you can, and then leave it. This is essentially what farmers used to do when they left a field fallow. You may be surprised by what sprouts up, for all soil contains a 'seed bank' of seeds that have been deposited in the past, some of them many years earlier. You might want to pull out any obvious weeds you do not want, such as nettles or docks, although of course these do have wildlife value. Mow your fallow patch in September, and otherwise you need do nothing. You almost certainly won't end up with anything terribly similar to a hay meadow but, whatever you get, I would wager that all sorts of interesting insect life will move in.

Alternatively, sow a meadow-seed mix in early autumn or spring. Again, many mixes are available commercially, and I have recommended a selection of suitable meadow flowers for different conditions at the end of this chapter. The optimum mixture depends on the soil type, drainage and shading. As with the 'growbag meadow', you might wish to include some colourful cornfield annuals such as poppy and cornflower to provide lots of colour and interest for bees in the first year.

To prepare the ground for your seeds, you can dig over the patch as above, removing weeds by hand, or you might cover the patch with a weed-proof membrane for a couple of months; black plastic sheeting or an old carpet will do the job. Then rake the surface to produce a fine tilth, and sprinkle on your seed. Trample it in to ensure that the seeds are in contact with the soil, and water well. Again, pull out any obvious weeds as they emerge. This approach usually works pretty well, although if you have damp weather soon after the seeds are germinating, then slugs may destroy all but the most unpalatable of the seedlings. With luck, by the summer you will have a profusion of flowers.

Just as with a hay meadow, patches such as this should be cut in late summer, and the cuttings removed. The flower community you create will change over time, and in a garden situation it is likely that you will lose many of the flowers as they are squeezed out by grasses and weeds. You may find that the best option is to simply repeat the whole process and re-sow the patch every three or four years.

Meadow creation option 4:
The full-scale meadow

This section is targeted at those lucky few readers who might have access to half an acre or more of land that they are willing to turn into their very own wildflower meadow. The first issue to consider is the fertility of the site. If the soil is too fertile then simply preparing a seed bed and sowing wildflower seeds will probably not work well in the long term. The high fertility will encourage weeds and grasses, which will quickly dominate and squeeze out the more desirable plants. If you suspect that this may be the case, you can get your soil tested by a commercial lab (see 'Useful addresses'). Phosphorus levels are most important, as high levels of phosphates favour fast growth of grasses. Ideally, the phosphorus index of your chosen site will be zero or 1; if it is higher than 2 then you have a problem (sometimes soil test results are quoted in mg/l, in which case a value over 20 is too high). If you can't afford to have the soil tested, just looking at the existing vegetation gives strong clues. If there are abundant nettles, docks, hogweed, or tall tussocky grasses such as false oat-grass (*Arrhenatherum elatius*) and cock's foot (*Dactylis glomerata*), then your soil is likely to be too fertile and you would be wise to take steps to reduce it. This can be done in a number of ways:

a) The most fertile soil is usually near the surface, so stripping off the top 5 cm is an effective way of reducing fertility. Ideally, find a home for the soil, as it would be a terrible shame to put good topsoil into a landfill. It can be offered on Freecycle, or used to create raised vegetable or ornamental flower beds.

b) Rather than getting rid of the topsoil, deep-ploughing can be used to bury it deep underground, along with the roots and seeds of weeds. This does require specialist ploughing equipment, which flips the soil profile over, although it can be replicated with a spade and a lot of sweat. If doing it by hand, dig a trench 40 cm deep, then take the top 20 cm from the adjacent strip and put it in the bottom of the trench, covering it with soil from 20 to 40 cm down. Repeat the process across your plot, filling the final trench with inverted soil from the first one.

c) A slower approach is to cut the vegetation close to the ground every month through spring and summer for at least one year, removing all the cuttings. Every cut removes some of the nutrients. This works very well on sandy soils which store few nutrients, but takes much longer on clay soils which cling on to phosphates and nitrates.

d) A similar practice is to sow and harvest crops for one or two years, without adding any fertiliser; the removed crop takes away the nutrients. Nutrient-hungry crops such as potatoes or brassicas are best. If the problem is particularly high phosphorus, then adding some nitrogen-rich fertiliser will help the crop grow and boost absorption of phosphorus.

As a final step before sowing a wildflower seed mix, it is common practice to use a systemic weedkiller such as glyphosate to eradicate pernicious weeds, but there are serious concerns about the environmental impacts of such chemicals, and I do not recommend their use. If nutrient levels have been addressed, then weeds should have low vigour and not be able to dominate, so a herbicide should not be necessary.

For sowing, a seed bed must first be prepared. If it is a large-scale operation this is usually done by harrowing and rolling, the aim being to provide a smooth, crumbly surface. On a smaller scale, a rotovator will do the job, or else you face the backbreaking challenge of shallow digging and then raking the surface.

Selecting a seed mix should be done with care, reflecting as far as possible the characteristics of the site and the soil type. The quantity of wildflower seed needed for large projects is considerable and the cost is significant, so it is best to avoid mistakes. Suggested plants suitable for different soil conditions are provided at the end of the chapter. If you can locate a flower-rich grassland near to your project and on similar soil then you'd be wise to take note of which species thrive there, as these are likely to be the most suitable for you.

Commercial suppliers of wildflower seed provide ready-made mixes suitable for particular conditions, and are usually happy to adapt the mix to your preferences, particularly if it's a sizeable project.

If your seed mix contains clovers, sainfoin or bird's-foot trefoil, check that the seeds are 'wild-type'. There are commercial strains of these species that have been selected for tall and rapid growth, often polyploidy varieties (having extra sets of chromosomes) that are much chunkier that their wild relatives. Seeds of these strains are much cheaper than the ones from wild-type plants, but they are not suitable for wildflower meadows since they tend to be short-lived.

The optimum time to sow your mix is September: at this time of year some wild flowers will germinate straight away, while others require the cold of winter before they germinate in early spring. The second-best option is to sow in April, but plants like yellow rattle that require chilling will not germinate until the following year, if at all. After sowing, the seeds should be rolled or raked to bring them into firm contact with the soil.

There is a much cheaper and more attractive alternative to buying and sowing a seed mix that with luck may be available. If there is an existing flower-rich grassland nearby, perhaps in a nature reserve, then it's worth contacting the landowner to see if they are willing to let you take some 'green hay'. Traditional hay-meadow management is to cut in late July or August. This fresh green hay can be immediately transported to your site and strewn across the prepared seed bed. As it dries, the ripening seeds will drop into the soil. Allowing cattle to trample it in, or running a roller over it, also helps get the seed into the soil. It is vital that the hay is transported and spread within a few hours as otherwise, if left in a large pile, it will start to compost and the seeds inside will be cooked.

Using green hay has big advantages; the species present are likely to be ones that will thrive in your conditions, and the seeds will be of local provenance and hence should be well adapted to your environment. What's more, green hay is usually cheap, or even free, for if the donor site is managed by an organisation that promotes nature conservation it will often be pleased to help. The only disadvantage is simply that there may not be a suitable donor site, or the owners may not wish to help.

No matter how carefully you have prepared your meadow, there are likely to be some weed problems in the early years, and usually it is a good idea to give the vegetation a high cut (with blades set at around 10 cm) two or three times from mid-July onwards for the first two years, and remove the cuttings. This removes more nutrients, prevents weeds such as thistles from setting seed, and allows the perennial wild flowers to fill out and become established.

From then on, you should be able to manage the meadow as one would an ancient hay meadow. Take a single cut each year in late July or August, leave the hay *in situ* to dry, and turn it at least once before collection. This allows the seeds to ripen and fall out. If this is not done, plants such as yellow rattle will disappear. If you wish to maintain good hay yields in the long term – for example, if you need the hay to feed livestock – then adding a small amount of well-rotted manure each year is acceptable, but obviously no synthetic fertilisers, or you will ruin all your hard work.

If it is possible, grazing in spring and/or autumn helps keep grasses down, and provides some bare patches where flower seed can germinate. Cattle are generally preferred to sheep because they'll happily browse on coarse and tussocky grasses, whereas sheep are more inclined to nibble out the leaves and buds of flowers. If no animals are available, or adequate fencing is not in place, then an additional spring hay cut is sometimes beneficial.

Cutting the hay in summer feels like sacrilege, as many plants are still in full flower and a meadow is alive with buzzing insects. The butterflies and bees are forced to flee, and many less mobile insects such as grasshoppers and crickets must surely perish. I console myself that, if it was not done, the home of these insects would eventually disappear. However, there is a way to mitigate the damage, which is to leave a corner or strip of the meadow uncut until September. The more mobile wildlife will move into the uncut area and, by the time the September cut comes, the main part of the meadow will have started to spring back up. Each year it is best to leave a different part of the meadow uncut until September.

Pollinator-friendly species suitable for wildflower-meadow seed mixes

Every plant species thrives best in particular conditions, particularly with regard to the soil type. While a few species, such as meadow buttercup, seem able to cope with almost any conditions, most are not so adaptable, and you would be wasting your time and money if you were to sow them in the wrong conditions. The table below indicates which species of meadow flower are best suited to particular soil types.

	Neutral	Alkaline, e.g. chalk	Slightly Acidic	Damp
Autumn hawkbit *Scorzoneroides autumnalis*	●			●
Betony *Stachys officinalis*	●	●	●	●
Bird's-foot trefoil *Lotus corniculatus*	●	●	●	
Bugle *Ajuga reptans*				●
Bulbous buttercup, *Ranunculus bulbosus*	●	●		
Bush vetch, *Vicia sepium*	●	●	●	●
Cat's-ear *Hypochaeris radicata*	●			
Common knapweed *Centaurea nigra*	●	●	●	●
Common toadflax, *Linaria vulgaris*	●			
Common vetch *Vicia sativa*	●			
Cowslip *Primula veris*	●	●	●	●
Cuckoo flower *Cardamine pratensis*				●
Devil's-bit scabious *Succisa pratensis*	●			●
Dropwort *Filipendula vulgaris*		●		
Field scabious *Knautia arvensis*	●	●		
Fleabane *Pulicaria dysenterica*				●
Greater bird's-foot trefoil *Lotus pedunculatus*				●
Greater knapweed *Centaurea scabiosa*		●		
Harebell *Campanula rotundifolia*		●		
Hemp agrimony *Eupatorium cannabinum*	●			

Table continued overleaf

	Neutral	Alkaline, e.g. chalk	Slightly Acidic	Damp
Horseshoe vetch *Hippocrepis comosa*		●		
Kidney vetch *Anthyllis vulneraria*		●		
Meadow buttercup *Ranunculus acris*	●	●	●	●
Meadow clary, *Salvia pratensis*	●	●	●	
Meadowsweet *Filipendula ulmaria*			●	●
Meadow vetchling *Lathyrus pratensis*	●		●	●
Musk mallow, *Malva moschata*	●	●		
Ox-eye daisy *Leucanthemum vulgare*	●	●	●	●
Ragged robin *Lychnis flos-cuculi*			●	●
Red clover *Trifolium pratense*	●	●	●	●
Rough hawkbit *Leontodon hispidus*	●	●		
Sainfoin, *Onobrychis viciifolia*		●		
Selfheal *Prunella vulgaris*	●		●	●
Small scabious *Scabiosa columbaria*		●		
St John's wort *Hypericum perforatum*	●			
Tufted vetch *Vicia cracca*	●	●		●
Viper's bugloss *Echium vulgare*	●	●		
Water avens *Geum rivale*				●
Wild basil *Clinopodium vulgare*		●		
Wild carrot *Daucus carota*	●	●		
Wild marjoram *Origanum vulgare*	●	●		
Wild thyme *Thymus polytrichus*		●		
Yarrow *Achillea millefolium*	●	●	●	●
Yellow rattle *Rhinanthus minor*	●	●	●	●

CHAPTER TWELVE

Providing Nest Sites for Bees

Among the most popular and reliable wildlife-gardening products are nest boxes for birds. Almost every wildlife garden contains at least one, and often several, with slightly different designs favouring blue tits, sparrows or robins. Tits in particular use these boxes very frequently, and we all love watching the parents busily to-ing and fro-ing as they build their nests and raise their chicks. Not surprisingly, bees need homes too, and the last decade or so has seen 'bee hotels' in a proliferation of designs appear on the garden-centre shelves. Before you rush out and buy some expensive, twee-looking box with a slate-tiled roof, I should warn you: many of them simply don't work. It is also very easy to make your own, with just some basic tools and for minimal cost. So let's look first at what bees might want in a home.

Bumblebees

In late winter or early spring, bumblebee queens emerge from their long hibernation and hungrily feed to replace their depleted fat reserves. They then turn their attention to finding a nest, and this is one of the most challenging parts of their life cycle. If they don't find a nest site, or choose one that is unsuitable, they are doomed.

All bumblebees need a large, dark cavity in which to nest; depending on the species, this cavity should be anywhere between a large orange and that of a shoe box in size, ideally with a small entrance just big enough for the queen to squeeze in and out. In nature, most bumblebee nests are underground, although a few species such as the common carder bumblebee prefer to nest under leaf litter just above the soil surface. Bumblebees are poor diggers and can't dig out their own nest, so they rely on mice, rats, moles, rabbits or people to make the excavation for them. In woodlands, old pastures and hedge-bottoms there must be immense networks of inter-connecting underground tunnels and chambers made by generations of burrowing mammals, and it is these that most bumblebees use. In gardens they may use animal burrows, but will also opportunistically occupy a diversity of man-made cavities – for example, under decking or patio slabs, in cavity walls, which they may enter via air-bricks, or under the wooden floor of garden sheds. Cavities in old compost heaps seem to be particularly attractive, presumably because the warmth provided by the composting process helps keep them cosy. One species, the tree bumblebee (*Bombus hypnorum*), is very happy to use tit boxes. This species wasn't recorded in the UK until 2001, when it somehow hopped the Channel, but has since become one of the UK's commonest garden bumblebees. Its success may in part be because we have inadvertently provided it with lots of 'bird' boxes to nest in. The tree bumblebee also very commonly nests under the insulation in lofts, entering via any crack it can find in the fascia boards; I have at least one nest in my loft most years.

Several types of bumblebee nest box are available commercially but, having tried dozens over many years, I can say that most designs are rarely if ever used by bumblebees (although if they were marketed as woodlouse, earwig and spider boxes they could claim to be highly effective). Most consist of something that looks similar to a wooden tit box: rectangular, designed to sit on the ground, and with an entrance hole drilled in one side. Having an entrance hole in a smooth vertical wall makes it hard for bumblebee queens of most species to access the box; generally the bees like to land near the hole and explore it on foot, so a hole at ground level is ideal, but many designs do not have this. A softwood box sitting on the soil inevitably rots within a small number of years, usually long before any bumblebees have shown an interest, so these boxes are usually a waste of money.

There are two commercially available boxes that seem to work much better. Schwegler nest boxes are a German design made from wood-concrete, a more or less indestructible and breathable material (available from NHBS, the Natural History Book Service: see 'Useful Addresses'). The entrance has a ledge beneath it for bumblebees to land on, which seems to work. They are chunky, heavy and expensive, but they often get bumblebees nesting in them, as long as suitable nesting material is provided (see below).

The second is a wooden nest box design developed by Nurturing Nature, a small company specialising in quality wildlife products (see 'Useful Addresses'). These set the entrance hole into a sloping, rather than vertical, wall, making it easier for prospective occupants to enter, and also have a clever entrance flap which the bees learn to use but which keeps out wax moths (harmful pests of bumblebee nests).

Schwegler nest box

Nurturing Nature nest box

If you don't want to spend lots of money on buying a ready-made nest box, it is pretty easy to make cavities that bumblebees might nest in, and a few possible designs are suggested here. I should warn you that, more often than not, they are not occupied by bumblebees but, if they aren't, they often provide homes for other creatures, including toads, voles, mice and shrews, beetles and spiders, and the inevitable woodlice, so your efforts will be appreciated by somebody. Feel free to try whatever you like – be creative! All sorts of designs are possible, making use of old bricks, stones, or pieces of timber.

Ideally, the nests should be sited in a sheltered spot along a 'linear feature' (a hedge, bank, wall or fence), for this seems to be where one most commonly sees queen bumblebees looking for places to nest in spring. The simplest design simply involves digging a hole approximately the size of a half-deflated football, and covering it with a paving slab or sheet of plywood, leaving a crack or two around the side for bees to get in and out and to provide a little ventilation. If you have an existing patio, you could simply lift a slab or two in a quiet corner and excavate a hole beneath. I have had white-tailed and buff-tailed bumblebees occupy this type of nest chamber. However you make a nesting cavity, good drainage is key. Try to avoid locations that might flood in a summer storm, since this is a common cause of bumblebee-nest failure. A dry, well-drained location with some ventilation is ideal as, aside from flooding, bumblebee nests can get mouldy if too damp.

Some books recommend using an upturned terracotta pot: cover the drainage hole with a tile or slate, and leave a gap under the edge for the bees to squeeze in and out. I have not yet had success with this method – there seems to be a lot of luck involved – but there is no harm in trying it.

Some bumblebee species prefer an entrance tunnel – 18 mm in diameter or more and 30–50 cm long. They will happily go further: I once attempted to excavate a buff-tailed bumblebee nest, and followed the winding, horizontal tunnel for about 8 metres until it disappeared under a tarmac pavement. Presumably nests at the end of long tunnels are safer from predatory badgers, which often dig up nests near the surface. To make an artificial tunnel to your nest chamber, any old bit of hose or pipe will do. A pin or nail across the centre of the entrance will discourage large snails and slugs from blocking the tunnel (they seem surprisingly prone to, and I have had bumblebee colonies expire because they were trapped in their nest by a large slug). Small drainage holes will prevent water pooling in the tube. In addition to their standard above-ground wood-concrete nest boxes, Schwegler manufacture one model intended to be buried in the ground and accessed by an integral tunnel, though I have not tried it.

Whether your nest is above or below ground, it seems to help if you make the entrance hole appear as natural as possible. Covering the hole with a slate or tile to create a shady overhang seems to attract nest-searching queens, and also helps keep out the rain. George Pilkington of Nurturing Nature uses a short entrance tube with his nest boxes, which he cunningly disguises by packing moss around it to give the appearance of a natural hole in a mossy bank.

Whatever design of nest box you make or buy, bedding is key. The biggest flaw of most commercial bumblebee nest boxes is that they come without appropriate bedding or advice as to how to create it. Queen bumblebees are very particular when it comes to such things, and without a comfy bed they will turn their nose up and depart. Coarse hay, sometimes supplied as standard in commercial boxes, is useless. Naturally, bumblebees use an old, cosy nest made by a small mammal, commonly consisting of a snug ball of finely woven grass stems lined with moss and hairs. An old bird's nest, lined with feathers, is also just the job. The queen will rearrange and remodel the materials to her liking, combing it with her bristly legs, but unless you give her the right basic materials you are wasting your and her time.

Hamster bedding (kapok) is an ideal substitute for a vole's or bird's nest. Upholsterer's cotton, freely available on the Internet, is also excellent. If you can tease this into a cosy ball with a hollow centre, mimicking the nest of a small mammal, so much the better. If the nest material is to rest on soil, first put in some twigs or a chicken-wire cradle to lift it clear of the ground. This will help stop it getting damp.

There is some debate as to whether it may help if you add some mouse droppings or material from an old mouse or vole nest to your nest bedding. Bumblebees have a poorly understood relationship with small mammals, for they rely on them to provide tunnels and abandoned nests, but conversely many small mammals such as wood mice probably depredate bumblebees, particularly their brood. It has long been suspected that bumblebees may use the smell of mice or voles themselves, or of their droppings or urine, as a cue for finding a cosy nest. If you have access to rodent bedding, perhaps from pet mice, gerbils or hamsters, it might be worth sprinkling a little into your nest cavity. I have tried using mouse bedding, but so far without noticeable effect. Alternatively, coaxing mice to live in your bumblebee nest over the winter by baiting it with peanut butter might help. On the other hand, given that some mammals are probably predators of bumblebee brood, the queen bees might avoid places which have been very recently occupied. Perhaps they can smell the difference between a disused mouse nest and one that is currently occupied? Do they prefer the smell of particular types of small mammal nest? We do not know, but there is certainly scope for the keen amateur to find out more about this and other aspects of how best to tempt bumblebee queens to occupy artificial nests.

Solitary bees

Most of the UK's 270 bee species are solitary: unlike bumblebees and honey bees, a female bee single-handedly makes her own nest. She has no workers, and there is no queen. Given that there are so many species of solitary bee, it is perhaps no surprise that they nest in lots of different places. The majority, including a large family known as mining bees (*Andrena*), tend to burrow into the ground. Unlike bumblebees they happily excavate their own holes, often leaving a neat spoil heap, a tell-tale cone of soil grains next to or surrounding their hole. Some ground-nesting bees such as the sharp-collared furrow bee (*Lasioglossum malachurum*) prefer to dig their nests in bare patches of ground, while others like the tawny mining bee will happily nest in lawns. Although they are solitary, many ground-nesting bees such as the ivy bee prefer to nest near one another in nesting 'aggregations', though whether this is because there is safety in numbers, or because these locations are particularly good for nesting, or simply because offspring tend to show fidelity to the place where they were born, is not clear.

It is not very easy to deliberately encourage ground-nesting bees. I have experimented with leaving patches of ground bare, but they are rarely occupied. In the countryside, ground-nesting bee nests tend to be along the edge of vehicle tracks, where the soil is somewhat compressed, but this is hard to replicate in a garden. Some bee species prefer to nest in sandy soils, and can be attracted to nest by leaving a heap of sand (at my house in France an abandoned pile of builder's sand is now home to many solitary bees, along with egg-laying wall lizards and green lizards).

The solitary bees most easily encouraged to use artificial 'bee hotels' are mason bees and their kin – species that naturally nest in horizontal holes. In nature they might use holes in trees left by wood-boring insects, the hollowed-out stems of pithy plants like bramble, or they might burrow into clay cliffs and banks. In the modern, tidy world they probably struggle to find many natural nesting sites, partly because dead trees aren't often left to decay and be consumed by burrowing insects. Soft lime mortar in an old brick wall does very nicely for some mason bee species, and some old houses have large populations of them burrowing in their walls. They very slowly weaken the mortar as they carve out their tiny homes, but my guess is that it would take centuries to do significant damage.

These days every garden centre sells at least one type of bee hotel aimed at solitary bees, and dozens of models are available online. Some work well but, as with bumblebee boxes, there are many duff ones on the market that are designed to look pretty to humans but of little interest to bees. Many are made from bundles of short lengths of bamboo squeezed into some sort of wooden box or tube, or holes drilled into a block of wood. There is nothing wrong with either approach, but often these designs are let down by the detail. It is common to see holes that are far too large: if they are bigger than about 12 mm then bees will generally not be interested, for they prefer a snug fit. Many designs are too shallow, meaning bees can squeeze very few offspring into each tube; ideally tubes should be at least 10 cm deep. If made from bamboo, it is common for the tubes to be blocked at the nodes; these should be drilled out. Often the bamboo is not cut neatly, or the drilled holes have frayed edges, making it hard for bees to enter and potentially damaging their wings as they go back and forth. In some commercial designs the holes are not sealed at the rear end, which again deters most potential residents.

Given these many shortcomings, there is a lot to be said for making your own bee hotel. This requires only simple, readily available tools, and very little in the way of DIY experience.

Design 1: *Bamboo canes*

Obtain bamboo canes with internal hole dimensions of 5–10 mm. Red mason bees (*Osmia bicornis*) are often the most abundant occupants of bee hotels, and they seem to prefer holes of around 8 mm diameter, so aim for some close to this. Cut the bamboo into equal-length pieces of 15 to 30 cm in length. Clear out any blockages within the holes with a drill and appropriately sized drill bit. Cut a length of plastic drainpipe to about 1 cm longer than the canes, and seal one end of the drain pipe with duct tape. Pack the canes into the pipe so that the end of the pipe overhangs the canes by 1 cm (the small overhang helps keep rain out of the tubes). Attach the pipe in a horizontal position to a wall, fence or post, either using a drainpipe bracket, or by wrapping coat-hanger wire around it and securing the wire to the wall with a screw. Alternatively, you can use an empty tin can instead of a piece of drainpipe, and supplement or replace the bamboo with other hollow-stemmed plants, such as reeds, hogweed or *Leycesteria*. If you don't have drainpipe or a tin can to put them in, you can just tie bundles of bamboo together with strong twine.

Bee hotels seem to work best if attached firmly to a wall or fence, preferably in a sunny position. Avoid attaching them to a tree, as they often become infested with earwigs, and avoid dappled shade if possible, as this seems to put the bees off. The height doesn't seem to matter much: I have had success with them anywhere between 30 centimetres and 3 metres above the ground.

Design 2: *Holes in a block of wood*

This could not be easier. Simply obtain any sizeable block of wood and drill as many horizontal holes into it as your enthusiasm allows. Change the drill bit occasionally, making lots of 8 mm diameter holes and a few of 10 mm, 6 mm and 4 mm. Drill as deep as your drill and the block of wood allow (do not drill right through): the bees will happily go in up to 30 cm or more given the chance, and the deeper the hole the more offspring they can pack in. Try to make sure the holes are clean, without splinters or other blockages. Screw the block of wood to a sturdy support as above.

Alternatively, you can simply drill holes in any wooden structure already in your garden, such as fence posts, a dead tree, or the corner posts of your garden shed.

Perhaps surprisingly, the holes don't need to be round: an alternative approach is to use a router to cut parallel grooves in a series of planks and then strap them together in a bundle. The resulting flat-sided or square holes seem to be perfectly acceptable to bees.

Less permanent but seemingly acceptable bee accommodation can be made by simply poking holes with a pencil in a block of 'Oasis' foam – the stuff used by florists. Mason bees will also nest in cardboard tubes or paper straws, as long as they are housed in a weather-proof container so they don't get soggy. I've seen mason bees seemingly happily nesting in plastic and glass tubes too, but the lack of breathability is suspected to make the grubs susceptible to mould, so this is probably best avoided.

One advantage of some commercial designs of bee hotel that is a bit more complicated to replicate with a DIY construction is that they have a viewing door opening onto a Perspex window, through which one can see what is happening inside the tunnels. This is fascinating, and a great way to engage children. In mason bees, the mother places a pile of bright yellow pollen in the bottom of the hole – just enough to feed the single egg that she lays on top – and then seals the cell up by building a wall of mud. Once the first cell is complete she starts again, eventually creating a neat row of cells, each containing one egg or developing white grub. As with most insects,

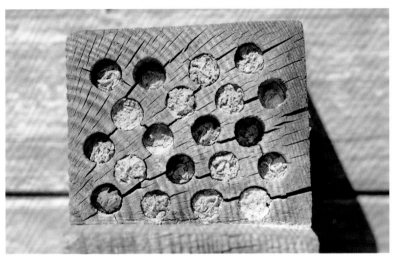

Top: Bee hotel, full

Middle: Inside bee hotel

Bottom: Mason bee and Ruby-tailed wasp

the males prefer to emerge before the females, so they are well placed to grab and mate with the young females when they emerge, and so the mother cleverly lays female eggs in the bottom of the tunnel and male eggs on top. Oddly, the bees seem little concerned by having the viewing window on the nest open, continuing about their business inside their nest despite being in daylight.

Unlike honey bees and bumblebees, which travel kilometres from their nests in search of food, solitary bees prefer to stay within a few hundred metres of home, and so need both nearby flowers and, in the case of mason bees, access to mud. If you are really keen to encourage your mason bees you could place a seed tray filled with moistened, clayey soil near the hotel, or dig a hole so they can easily get access to the damp soil. I use an old broken wheelbarrow into which I shovel the soil from a molehill, dampened with a little water. The female bees eagerly collect the mud, forming it into a ball that they carry in their jaws.

In addition to red mason bees, if you are lucky your hotel may also attract the slightly smaller blue mason bee (*Osmia caerulescens*), which plugs its nest entrance with a dark, grey-green mastic made from chewed leaves. Most mason bees are active early in the spring, but as the year progresses other solitary bees and wasps may turn up too. Smaller holes will encourage yellow-faced bees (*Hylaeus* species), slim yellow-and-black mason wasps (*Eumeninae*, which stock their nests with caterpillars), or even smaller red-and-black *Sphecidae* wasps (which tend to stock their nests with aphids, tiny flies or spiders). Bigger holes of about 9 or 10 millimetres' diameter are preferred by leafcutter bees, which need the extra room as they line their chosen burrow with semi-circles of leaves that they cut out with their mandibles, and sew together with silk.

These bees and wasps then attract other interesting beasts, including cuckoo bees such as the sharp-tailed bee, which dashes in and lays eggs in the nests of leafcutter bees. There are also parasitoid wasps that lay their eggs in or on the developing bee larvae, such as the wild carrot wasp (*Gasteruption jaculator*), the female of which bears an egg-laying tube longer than her entire body that she uses to drill down through the mud plug of mason bees into the unfortunate grubs beneath. You might also glimpse stunningly beautiful ruby-tailed wasps (*Chrysididae*), iridescent green-and-purple insects that sneak into the nests of solitary bees and wasps where their young feed on the food stores and the host's offspring. Some of these creatures are much rarer than their hosts, and that they are harming our bees does not, to my mind, mean we should discourage them.

If woodpeckers frequent your garden you might also consider protecting your bee hotel from them. Woodpeckers will pull out bamboo canes and cardboard tubes from their housing, and use their long tongue to hook out the grubs inside. It is very hard to keep them out, as they are surprisingly powerful, but chicken wire or wire mesh over the hotel can help. On the other hand, personally I am quite happy to see a few mason bees consumed, and to think that some of the bee-friendly flowers I grow ultimately help to feed these attractive birds. I have lots of different bee hotels dotted around, some with deep holes drilling in lumps of oak, so that at least some of the bee grubs are beyond the reach of woodpeckers.

Although most people would accept that woodpeckers need food too, and that ruby-tailed wasps and sharp-tailed bees deserve their place in the world, it is interesting that most of us are less generous when it comes to the mites, fungi and bacteria that also attack our bees. For example, bees suffer from infestation by many different mites (distant relatives of spiders), some so tiny that they cannot be seen with the naked eye. Under a microscope these squat, eight-legged creatures are, to most humans, quite revolting to behold. The most common ones on mason bees are pollen mites, which hitch a ride on the adult bees and then jump off into the pollen stores in the nest. Sometimes bees can be heavily infested, their bodies smothered in thousands of tiny mites, so that they spend much time trying to groom them off. Although it makes my skin crawl to see them, the mites do not actually feed upon or directly harm the bee, other than by weighing it down.

Once in the pollen store, it is a race between the bee grub and the mites to eat the food. If there aren't too many mites, the grub usually gets most of the food and grows big enough to pupate successfully. In a heavy mite infestation, or if the bee grub is diseased or doesn't develop for other reasons, the mites proliferate and fill the mud-lined cell with tens of thousands of offspring. In a bee hotel with viewing windows these cells are obvious in autumn – instead of a chocolate-brown cocoon, the cell appears to contain a dense mass of pinkish-brown spores, each a dormant mite waiting for its chance to infest a new mason bee nest. Any bee emerging from deeper in the tunnel in the spring has to crawl through this mass of tiny parasites, and inevitably becomes heavily infested, continuing the cycle.

It is more-or-less impossible to stop pollen mites from infesting your bee hotels. The mites jump from bee to bee during mating, and will also jump off onto flowers and wait for another bee to come along, so most mason bees have some mites on them. A large bee hotel left *in situ* for a few years will inevitably contain many mites, and it can sometimes reach the point where few bee offspring survive and the bee population collapses.

If you are really keen to maximise your mason bee population and control the mites, you need a bee hotel that can be dismantled and disinfected in winter. This is impossible with those constructed from bamboo or holes in solid wood, but can be done with some commercial designs such as Nurturing Nature's, and with home-made designs in which grooved planks of wood are strapped together. These can be taken apart in autumn or winter, and the bee cocoons gently removed and left somewhere safe, cool and dark until spring. The hotel itself can then be sterilised with boiling water and hung back up, pristine, early in the spring.

Because of issues with the build-up of mites and also diseases, there is some debate as to whether bee hotels are actually beneficial to bees. Do they provide much-needed nest sites, boosting the bee pop-ulation, or do they lure them in to a crowded high-rise where they are doomed to become parasitised and diseased? At present nobody knows, and this is something that certainly needs more study. In the meantime, my best guess is that bee hotels are doing more good than harm, particularly if one considers wider biodiversity and not just populations of mason bees. I avoid making the giant bee hotels I have sometimes seen, and instead scatter small ones around my garden. Some are commercial ones I have been given as presents, but most are simple home-made designs. I sometimes just wander around my garden with a cordless electric drill and make a few holes in any piece of wood I can find. My main compost heap is made from several old wooden pallets, and I've drilled holes in the corners of those, as well as in various logs scattered about. As a strategy it seems to work: they are not all occupied at the same time, but in my garden I have good populations of various bees, wasps, mites, and probably bee diseases too, along with a pair of fat great spotted woodpeckers, which seems to me how it should be.

CHAPTER THIRTEEN

Providing Breeding Sites for Other Pollinators

As I've mentioned, there is much more to the world of pollination than bees, lovely though they are. Other pollinators include hover-flies, butterflies, moths, beetles, many types of wasps, midges and thrips. One cannot make homes for all of them, and perhaps there is no need to try. It is the adults of these insects that pollinate flowers, and so by growing a range of pollinator-friendly flowers you will be keeping them content. However, the immature stages, the caterpillars, grubs, maggots or nymphs, feed on other things. In general, if you have a quiet corner or two, perhaps some long grass, a small pond, and use few or no pesticides, many of them will find conditions that suit them somewhere in your garden.

Butterflies and moths

The caterpillars of butterflies and moths tend to be fussy eaters, often only consuming a few closely related types of plant at most, and the female butterflies are very careful to seek out the correct food plant on which to lay their eggs. Famously, many of our prettiest common garden butterflies, such as the peacock and small tortoiseshell, lay their eggs on nettles. Unfortunately, they seem to prefer to lay on big patches of nettles in sunny situations, so even if you do encourage nettles in your garden it probably won't work in attracting butterflies unless you have room for a lot. If you are lucky enough to have a good-sized nettle patch, chop some of it back in early June, as the butterflies like to lay on fresh regrowth, which is scarce in midsummer (the cuttings make great liquid compost). Even if you fail to attract any butterflies to your nettles, do not despair, for nettles are also food for the caterpillars of about thirty species of moth, including beauties such as the burnished brass, garden tiger and angle shades, many of which will happily occupy even a small patch. Young nettle tops are also a great spinach substitute for us humans, though of course don't try eating them fresh.

Perhaps more appealing to most gardeners is to provide clovers and bird's-foot trefoil, which with luck will attract egg-laying common blue butterflies, the males with flashing, sky-blue wings, the females chocolate-brown with orange spots. Your cabbages are very likely to attract both large and small white butterflies, though you may wish they wouldn't. Cuckoo flowers might draw in orange tips, one of my favourite spring butterflies. A sunny meadow area may encourage meadow browns, gatekeepers, ringlets and skippers to breed, for their caterpillars feed on grasses. If you can leave a small patch of long grass uncut from one summer to the next you will give these butterflies the best chance to complete their development, for they spend most of the year as caterpillars feeding on the grass, and are hence vulnerable to cutting at any time apart from high summer, when the butterflies are flying.

If you have a shady garden with established trees you will be unlikely to attract meadow species, but if you leave a patch of long grass you might still be rewarded by the arrival of speckled wood butterflies. The adult males will often battle over sun spots, fighting ascending spiral battles in which they somehow agree on a winner and loser. In a wooded garden you will also stand a good chance of seeing holly blue butterflies: the caterpillars feed on the berries of mature holly and ivy. Grow a buckthorn bush and there is a reasonable chance you will attract brimstone butterflies.

Cuckoo flower   *Green longhorn moth*

Which butterflies you might attract to live with you in your garden depends to some extent on how close you are to a source population, but with only a little effort you should be able to attract at least half a dozen butterfly species to breed, even in an inner-city garden.

As for encouraging moths, there are so many different species (about 2,500 in the UK) that almost any native plant species you grow is bound to provide food for the caterpillars of at least one or two of them. Native shrubs and trees are particularly useful: a nice mixed hedge can support hundreds of moth species. If you have a large garden, a single oak tree will provide food for dozens of different types, including perhaps the green longhorn, a small day-flying metallic green moth with enormously long, white antennae that extend four times the length of its body.

Some great plants for pollinators serve the double purpose of providing food for moth caterpillars. Squeeze in some of the afore-mentioned bird's-foot trefoil and, as well as common blue butterflies, you might get burnet moth caterpillars. If you are lucky, willowherb or fuchsia will provide food for elephant hawkmoths, the larvae of which have large false eyes that make them resemble a small brown snake. Allow some ragwort to grow and you will very likely get the stripy orange-and-black caterpillars of cinnabar moths.

Even if their secretive habits mean you may never see most of the moths that live in your garden, it is great to provide homes for them, as their caterpillars are vital food for many wild birds such as great tits, and the adults provide food for both birds and bats.

Hoverflies

The larvae of hoverflies take a little while to grow to love. Being flies, their offspring are maggots: pale, limbless, wriggling creatures. Hoverfly larvae are often more or less transparent, so their internal organs are visible – not an attractive look in any organism. Nevertheless, these insects are of huge economic and biological importance, for the larvae of many hoverfly species are voracious predators of aphids. Despite the absence of limbs, they are able to climb nimbly up plants, even crawling across the undersides of leaves in search of their prey, which they seize with hooked mouthparts and suck dry. Providing flowers to attract adult hoverflies to your garden, and draw them close to your vegetable crops, is thus a great environmentally friendly way to control these pests.

Some other types of hoverfly larvae are aquatic: they naturally live in stagnant puddles, or rot-holes in trees where water and dead leaves have gathered in a shattered tree stump or the fork between large branches. Such places aren't as common as they used to be, as we tend to keep the landscape tidy and get rid of old, dead or dying trees. Luckily, it is easy to create artificial breeding habitats for these beasts, as Dr Ellie Rotheray at Sussex University, who did her PhD on hoverflies, discovered. Take-up rate for her artificial 'hoverfly lagoons' is high.

All you need is a waterproof container that will hold at least a litre of water. The size and shape don't seem to be particularly important: even a plastic milk carton with the top chopped off will work, though these do tend to disintegrate after a couple of years' exposure to sunlight. An old ceramic bowl, an unwanted saucepan or a child's plastic bucket will all work. Fill the container with cut grass or leaves and then stand a few twigs in it so they protrude from the top. Top up with rainwater to the brim, and put the container in a quiet corner of the garden where it won't get accidentally kicked over.

As the grass and leaves start to rot, bacteria and other microbes proliferate in the soupy water, and the smell attracts adult female flies to come and lay their clusters of eggs. In my garden, the tiger

Hoverfly   *Hoverfly larva*

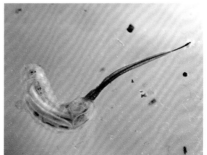

Hoverfly lagoon   *Rat-tailed maggot*

Hoverfly lagoons

261

hoverfly (*Helophilus pendulus*) is usually the first species to arrive, the males perching on the rim of the container or on the protruding twigs, from where they watch out for incoming females and the prospect of swift sex. When the water becomes really foetid, which only seems to happen if you add a large amount of fresh green foliage, various drone fly species appear (*Eristalis*). If you are lucky, you will soon spot clusters of white, sausage-shaped eggs laid on a protruding leaf of twig just above the water line, and soon afterwards, if you look very closely, you'll see tiny pale maggots, no bigger than a printed comma, floating just beneath the surface. In warm weather these larvae grow quickly, feasting on the bacterial soup in the water, and become fat yellowish-brown or creamy maggots, each equipped with a long, thread-like tail, commonly known as rat-tailed maggots.

Ellie has tried to rebrand them as 'long-tailed larvae', which sounds less repulsive. The tail is telescopic, and can stretch much longer than the length of the rest of the body. It is actually a breathing tube, a maggot snorkel, extending up to the surface to gather oxygen, since the stagnant water in rot holes is usually very low in this vital commodity. The long tail enables the larvae to keep their plump bodies well below the surface in the murky liquid, where predatory birds cannot easily see them. These hoverflies can go through several generations in a year, with larvae of various stages to be seen throughout the spring and summer, and some overwintering as larvae in the water.

When they are fully grown, the larvae shin up the protruding twigs placed there for this purpose, and drop down to the ground, where they transform into chocolate-brown pupae, still equipped with a long tail, which presumably by this stage is redundant. The pupae are rather endearing for, in addition to the tail, they have a pair of ear-like structures at the front which make them look a little like tiny mice. If you stand your lagoon in a container full of dead leaves or wood chips, with drainage holes in the bottom, then the larvae will tend to pupate here, and the pupae are easy enough to find.

At the time of writing we do not know much about which types of organic matter work best, or what is the optimal size or depth of lagoons, so there is plenty of scope for experimentation. It seems likely that the different hoverfly species that occupy these lagoons have different preferences, but this has not been investigated. If you would like to take part in a nationwide experiment to find out how to optimise hoverfly-lagoon design to get the most hoverflies in your garden, check out the Buzz Club (see 'Useful Addresses').

CHAPTER FOURTEEN

Pest Control

Sadly, the immediate response of many gardeners to seeing a few aphids on their roses, or spotting butterfly caterpillars munching the leaves of their cabbages, is to reach for an insecticidal 'bug' spray. In my opinion, these are far too readily available, since they can be purchased online, from any garden centre or DIY retail store, and even from ordinary supermarkets. Some of these products are potent toxins, and many are suspected or known carcinogens, yet they are freely sold to anyone, regardless of age or experience, and are then often applied without the user paying much or any attention to the instructions, sometimes without even the most basic protective gear such as rubber gloves. The manufacturers and retailers will tell you that these chemicals are all safe, but then forty years ago they told us that DDT was safe, and more recently that neonicotinoid insecticides didn't harm bees, but both claims proved far from the truth.

In a garden setting, there is absolutely no need for any chemical pesticides, and every reason to avoid them. Risks to yourself and your family aside, if you've planted flowers to attract and feed pollinators, the last thing you should do is spray them with chemicals that will poison the insects you attract. Many gardeners, including me, no longer use any pesticides, and we still seem to manage to grow plenty of flowers and tasty vegetables and fruits.

Even if you do not use pesticides yourself, you should be careful where you buy plants for your garden, as otherwise you may inadvertently bring home plants that have been drenched in pesticides. In 2016 my research group at Sussex University screened the pollen and nectar of plants being sold by garden centres as 'bee-friendly' or 'perfect for pollinators' (the Royal Horticultural Society badging), and found that almost all contained a cocktail of chemicals, including neonicotinoid insecticides. This is hardly 'perfect'. The only way, therefore, to be sure you are getting pesticide-free plants is to buy from an organic nursery (some are available online: see 'Useful Addresses'), propagate your own plants, or plant-swap with your friends.

To understand how pests can be managed without chemicals, it is worth taking another brief diversion into ecological theory. Natural ecosystems are usually diverse, with hundreds or thousands of species of plants, animals, fungi and bacteria involved in complex webs of interactions. Each flower species may be visited by dozens of different pollinators, nibbled by many different herbivores, and interact via its roots below the soil surface with a myriad of microbes, fungi and invertebrate animals. Diverse predators such as spiders, shrews, wrens and centipedes prey upon the herbivores, pollinators and soil-dwelling organisms. Numbers of each species are constrained by competition and predation. The ecosystem is in equilibrium and, although numbers of different species may vary over time, usually there are not wild fluctuations or devastating outbreaks of pests. Recent evidence suggests that, the more organisms involved in the web of interactions, the more stable it is; in ecologist's parlance, the system is more resilient to perturbations.

In contrast to natural systems, a large crop monoculture such as a field of wheat supports very few organisms. There is essentially no web of life, and therefore it is a hugely unstable system. If a pest arrives that likes to feed on wheat (as one inevitably does), it finds a sea of its favourite food with no natural enemies in sight. The pest reproduces, fast, and in no time at all the crop is infested. There may be some natural enemies that had been hanging out in the hedges, but with large fields there are never enough of them to spread quickly

Ladybird

into the field and control the pest. The farmer often feels he has no option but to spray a pesticide.

We can learn from this and, by some small adjustments to the way we garden, engineer it so that we have minimal pest problems.

First, in almost any garden you will already have a complex web of life, with hundreds of different species present. Gardens typically have much more diversity than arable fields, with a range of different herbaceous plants, grasses, shrubs and perhaps a pond and a tree or two. If you avoid pesticides, grow some pollinator-friendly plants and have a small meadow area, you will have literally thousands of species in your garden, which will include some pest species and also their various natural enemies. You may spot a few aphids on your roses or broad beans, but if you ignore them then sooner or later a ladybird, lacewing, soldier beetle or hoverfly larva will usually come along and eat them. The worst-case scenario is that you still have some aphids on your roses – is that really such a disaster? If you do resort to using an insecticide, you can expect worse pest problems in the very near future for, in addition to the pests, you will have also wiped out their natural enemies, and it is a characteristic of pest insects that their populations tend to recover much faster than those of their enemies.

Pesticides

If you have plants in your garden that are routinely attacked by heavy infestations of pests, this is a sure sign that the plant is not well. You may simply be trying to grow a plant that is not suited to your soil or local climate; for example, some plants such as blueberries will only thrive in acid soils. Try to grow them in neutral or alkaline soils and they will be stressed and susceptible to pests and diseases. You could grow them in pots with suitable acidic compost, or you could just grow something else, such as honeyberries, which taste much the same but are less fussy about their soil. Choosing plants that thrive in the conditions you have is the surest way to stress-free gardening, both for yourself and your plants.

In the vegetable garden, it is common practice to plant patches of particular crops, creating small-scale monocultures. Some vegetable crops are susceptible to pests: carrot to carrot fly, beans to blackfly, courgettes and lettuce to slugs. The impact of these pests can be reduced by using a number of simple techniques:

a) **Rotations.** Always ensure that you move your vegetable crops around each year, ideally not returning any crop to the same piece of ground more than once every four years – even longer if possible. This is particularly important for pests that live in the soil, such as potato cyst eelworm, which otherwise will build up year on year and soon reach a point where the crop is destroyed.

b) **Choose resistant varieties.** If you have recurring problems with a particular pest on a particular crop, explore whether there isn't a resistant variety available. For example, there are quite a few carrot varieties, such as the aptly-named 'Flyaway', which have high resistance to carrot root fly. Similarly, there are potatoes that are resistant to particular pests: 'Kestrel' is one of my favourites, having high resistance to slugs.

c) **Attract biocontrol agents.** Many natural enemies, such as parasitoid wasps, soldier beetles and hoverflies, need nectar and/or pollen. The tiny adult parasitic wasps that lay their eggs in aphids, for example, themselves need to feed upon flowers to develop their eggs, as do female hoverflies. Hence, growing the right kinds of flowers, such as French marigolds or umbellifers (*Apiaceae*), close to or among your vegetable crops is a great way to lure these predators to where they are needed. This approach is even used on a farm scale: in New Zealand, farmers commonly plant strips of *Phacelia* next to their cereal crops to attract predatory hoverflies. Natural enemies can also be encouraged by providing them with shelter. Earwigs, for example, are voracious predators of aphids, particularly in orchard settings, but they need safe places to hide in the day, and a string bag or tin can stuffed with straw and tied to a branch seems to be quite suitable.

d) **Mixed crops and companion plants.** Rather than planting blocks of vegetables, mixing them up (for example by alternating rows) seems to help reduce pest numbers. Most pest insects are specialists, feeding only on one type of crop, or a few closely related ones. They use the characteristic odour of their host plant to locate it, so mixing the susceptible crop with highly pungent plants makes that harder. In particular, the strong smell of onions (and their relatives such as leeks and garlic) planted among crops such as carrots and brassicas is thought to provide protection, and of course the onions themselves can be harvested, so no space is wasted. Similarly, French marigolds have strong-smelling foliage which can confuse or deter pests; I grow them amongst my tomatoes and find they help to keep whitefly away. Aromatic herbs such as rosemary, thyme, mint and basil are also said to have similar properties, although I have not found them to be so effective. Although companion planting has been used for centuries, and generations of experienced gardeners swear by it, it must be said that it has rarely been subject to rigorous scientific evaluation. In particular, the combinations of companion plants that work best have not been investigated in any systematic way, and we do not know the optimal ratios of different companion and crop plants, or what the best spatial arrangement to plant them in is. There is plenty of scope for home experimentation and discovery.

Companion planting   *Nasturtium trap crop*

e) **Trap crops.** Some plants are very attractive to pests, and will draw them away from your vegetables. I plant nasturtiums to attract blackfly away from broad and runner beans. The nasturtiums sometimes become heavily infested and look pretty awful, at which point they can be pulled up and buried in the compost heap, but I usually leave them to provide food for their many natural enemies.

f) **Physical protection.** Some pests are very easily deterred by netting. For example, the caterpillars of both small and large white butterflies can do tremendous damage to brassicas, but the adult female butterflies are easily kept at bay by light netting with holes of less than 2 cm diameter. Carrot fly are much smaller, and so fine netting or fleece is needed to keep them out, but they always fly low to the ground, so your carrots do not need to be completely covered; a 60 cm netting wall surrounding them will do the job.

Slugs

The pest I find to be most problematic is the slug. Unlike most insect pests, slugs are not specialists: they will happily eat most vegetable crops, although some, such as bean, curcubit and lettuce seedlings, seem to be their absolute favourites. They are also a problem almost everywhere, although shady gardens and those on heavy clay soils tend to be worse affected. I wish I could say that, if you leave them well alone and have a healthy, pesticide-free garden, natural enemies will take care of them, but usually this is not the case. I would be able to grow very few vegetables if I didn't do something to combat slugs. Many different control options are available, none of them ideal:

a) **Beer traps.** These are easily made from any plastic cup or old tin can, sunk partly into the ground and filled with a 50:50 mix of beer and water. Don't sink them so the edge is flush to the ground, as you risk drowning useful creatures like ground beetles. Rigging up a rain cover – for example using an old roof tile – helps to stop them flooding and the beer being washed away in heavy rain. Beer traps do certainly drown a few slugs, but on their own they do not seem to make much impact on the overall population.

b) **Hand searches.** If you are really dedicated, you can go out with a torch on damp nights and collect slugs up for 'disposal' (or simply execute them on the spot by chopping off their head with a sharp knife). This is obviously not a pleasant task, and doing it regularly is beyond the enthusiasm of most gardeners. Do not kill leopard slugs, *Limax maximus* (large grey slugs with black spots and streaks), for they are actually useful predators of the harmful slugs. In most gardens the biggest pest species is the grey field slug (*Deroceras reticulatum*), a medium-sized, blotchy, pale-grey slug with a milky mucus trail: this is the one to target with your decapitatory efforts. If you don't fancy creeping about in the dark on rainy nights, put cabbage leaves or the skins of grapefruit halves on the ground between your vegetables and slugs will often shelter under them, where they can be picked off in daylight hours.

c) **Encouraging predators.** Various predators will help keep slug numbers in check. Slow worms love to eat them – they are one of the very few creatures that prefer slugs over other food – but sadly I have no slow worms in my garden and they are rare these days, so it's unlikely that you will have them either. Placing a sheet of corrugated tin in an unshaded corner of your garden will tell you whether you are one of the lucky folk, for they love to warm up under tin sheets on sunny mornings, but there is little else you can do to encourage them, beyond the broad principles of having a floristically diverse and pesticide-free garden.

Hedgehogs also seem to enjoy munching slugs, but again you will be lucky if you have one in residence. If you have space I would recommend keeping some ducks: I have a small flotilla of Welsh harlequin and Indian runners that diligently search around in the leaf litter and undergrowth for slugs, wolfing them down and turning them into deliciously richly-flavoured (and not at all sluggy) duck eggs. The only downside of ducks is that they also eat frogs, and frogs (particularly the young ones) eat slugs too. Encouraging frogs and toads by having a small pond is likely to be a more practical option for most than keeping ducks.

Probably the most effective slug predators in most gardens are ground beetles (*Carabidae*): black, shiny, fast-running, nocturnal beetles that are partial to a midnight feast of slugs, and can be encouraged by providing a patch of long grass near your vegetables. This is a technique that has caught on in farming, whereby strips of tussocky grass known as 'beetle banks' are sown across big fields, proving a day-time hideaway for these nocturnal beetles.

d) **Slug barriers.** Surrounding seedlings with coffee grounds, crushed eggshells or ash from a fire all seem to be partially successful in my experience, but in really wet weather the slugs always seem to get through in the end. For particularly prized plants, rings of copper wire seem to be reasonably effective in all weathers, but it is difficult to devise a practical means of defending large numbers of plants in this way.

e) **Sacrificial plants.** I am not suggesting that you offer up some plants to the gods in exchange for protecting your crop, although this might be worth a try. Instead, you might grow something close to your vegetable patch that slugs find even more irresistible than your lettuce seedlings. Lawn camomile (*Chamaemelum nobile*) is said to be an absolute magnet for slugs, but it likes a well-drained soil, so I cannot keep it alive long enough for the slugs to eat it.

f) **Organic slug pellets.** These are made from ferric phosphate, a compound said to be much less harmful to wildlife than the metaldehyde used in conventional pellets. RHS trials suggest that these pellets do work, but there seems to be little convincing research demonstrating their safety or otherwise, so I prefer to avoid them.

g) **Nematodes.** This, in my experience, is the most effective and simplest form of slug control, albeit the most expensive. Nematodes are tiny, thread-like worms, and include many parasitic species that live in the guts of humans and other animals, and also species that are major pests of crops, such as the potato cyst nematode. One species, which revels in the unpronounceable name *Phasmarhabditis hermaphrodita*, is a specialist parasite of slugs, and is now commercially available for slug control. Sachets of powder containing young, microscopic nematodes can be bought, mixed with water, and sprinkled on to the area to be protected during warm, wet weather. These nematodes are available by mail-order, but I find it is better to purchase them from a garden centre, as ideally they should be kept refrigerated or at least cool before use, and this can't be guaranteed in the post. Fascinatingly, the nematode is tightly associated with a symbiotic bacterium. The young nematode burrows into its unfortunate host, infecting it with the bacterium, and it is the multiplication of the bacteria that eventually kills the slug. The nematode feasts on the bacterial soup inside the dying slug, and eventually more juvenile nematodes are produced and wriggle off through the soil in search of a fresh host. Revolting though all this sounds, the process is quite effective, and seems safe to all other organisms. The only drawback, aside from cost, is that the process has to be repeated every six weeks or so as the nematodes seem to die out.

When dealing with crop pests, it is also useful to bear in mind that some crop damage is inevitable, whatever you do. No method (including using pesticides) will give 100 per cent control. Small numbers of pests are a good thing, because they support populations of predators, and in any case many crops can tolerate a little damage without any reduction in yield. Despite planting nasturtiums to draw them away, in most years at least some of my broad beans become infested with black bean aphids. It can look awful, but I leave well alone and within a couple of weeks the cavalry arrives, in the form of a swarm of predatory insects. The aphids are wiped out, the crop recovers, and I get a great yield of pesticide-free beans. The predators then fan out through the vegetable patch, hoovering up any other aphids they can find. The interactions between the herbivores (pests) and their enemies are all part of a healthy garden ecosystem.

CHAPTER FIFTEEN

Where to Get Plants and Seeds

Gathering your own wildflower seeds

It is easy to collect your own seeds from the wild. Make sure the seeds are ripe when you collect them: ripe seeds are usually dark brown or black and hard, and readily detach from the flower head, while unripe seeds are pale, often cream, white or green, and soft. Of course you must not collect seeds of rare plants, or from protected areas such as nature reserves. Most of the wild flowers recommended here for pollinators can, with a little perseverance, be found on roadside verges, footpaths and field margins in much of the UK. You should not be racked with guilt (as some people are!) for collecting a few seeds from relatively common flowers. In nature the vast majority of seeds perish, since far more are produced than can possibly germinate, so there are plenty spare for the wildlife gardener. Collecting seed locally is not only the cheapest option, but also ensures that the species you are trying to grow are likely to thrive in your local soil type and climate. Moreover, even *within* plant species there can be local races and genotypes that are adapted to the particular local conditions. If you buy seeds from a commercial supplier they will probably originate from hundreds of miles away, sometimes from mainland Europe. These plants may not thrive in your area, and if they do you run the risk of polluting your local race with exotic genotypes.

If need be, seeds of most species will keep for a year or more if well dried, sealed in paper bags or envelopes, and kept in a cool dry place. Storing them in an old biscuit tin is wise, as otherwise they may be eaten by mice.

Longevity of seeds varies enormously between species. Poppy seeds, for example, can remain viable for decades, while parsnip seeds tend not to germinate if more than one year old. Since this kind of information is not readily available for most wild flower species, in general it is safest to sow hand-collected seeds immediately in seed trays, and then leave the trays in a cold frame or outside for the winter. Seeds of many native wild flowers will not germinate until they have been through a period of freezing, which tells them that winter has passed and spring is on the way.

Of course, you are unlikely to be able to collect your own wild-flower seeds of every species you might wish to grow. Luckily, a comprehensive range of wildflower seeds can be obtained from specialist suppliers, most of whom provide seeds by mail order complete with growing instructions. Websites for a selection of suppliers are listed below. Most of the big garden centre chains also sell wildflower seed and pot-grown wild flowers, but the selection is usually very limited. Unfortunately, specialist wild flower nurseries that are open to the public are few and far between.

Wildflower seed and plant suppliers online

Bee-Friendly Wild Flower Seeds

Attractively packaged bee- and butterfly-friendly seed mixes, ideal for gifts and wedding favours.

http://beefriendlyseeds.com

Bee Happy Plants

A knowledgeable and specialist company selling a broad range of wildflower seeds, including some very unusual plants, all selected specifically for their value to bees. Unusually, the seeds are reared entirely *organically*.

https://beehappyplants.co.uk

Cotswold Grass Seeds Direct

A long-established company selling bulk meadow mixes for different conditions and a good range of individual wild flower species.

https://www.cotswoldseeds.com/

Emorsgate Seeds

Specialist growers of UK wild flowers in bulk, Emorsgate is a very experienced company able to provide an extensive range of seed mixes tailored to different soils types and situations. I would recommend it if you are planning a large-scale meadow-restoration project. It has an extensive list of individual wild flower species, almost all of which are grown and harvested by Emorsgate on its own farms in the UK (not always the case with some other wildflower seed companies).

https://wildseed.co.uk/

Herbiseed

An international company with farms in the UK and abroad, specialising in growing and supplying unusual and specialist wildflower seeds, Herbiseed offers an extensive range of species and also tailored meadow mixes. It is probably most suitable as a supplier for large-scale meadow-restoration projects.

www.herbiseed.com

Naturescape

Specialist suppliers of UK wildflower seeds, meadow mixes and a big range of potted wild flower plants ready to plant out in the garden. It also supplies native shrubs and trees, and pond plants.

www.naturescape.co.uk

Organic Gardening Catalogue

A small selection of wildflower seeds and meadow mixes, plus fruit and vegetable seeds and plants, and a small selection of fruit trees, all reared *organically.*

https://www.organiccatalogue.com/seeds/wild-flower-seeds/
wild-flower-single-species/

rosybee: plants for bees

A delightful specialist supplier of plants that are attractive to bees, with a very informative and helpful website that includes its own research into which plants are preferred by different types of bee. All plants are guaranteed to be *pesticide-free,* and are grown without peat, so this is a great ethical choice.

http://www.rosybee.com

Scotia Seeds

Ideally, one should always try to buy seeds of local provenance, as these will be best suited to the local area. Hence, if you are sowing wildflower seeds or meadow mixes in Scotland you would be wise to head for Scotia Seeds, to my knowledge the only company selling seeds specifically of Scottish provenance. It sells a range of individual wild flowers, plus seed mixes tailored to a range of Scottish environments.

www.scotiaseeds.co.uk

Suppliers of fruit trees and soft fruits

Adam's Apples

Over 130 varieties of apple trees, including some rare West-Country varieties, available on a range of different rootstocks, plus other fruit trees and soft fruit. Reduced prices for bulk purchase.

Egremont Barn, Payhembury, Honiton, Devon, EX14 3JA

www.talatonplants.co.uk

Agroforestry Research Trust

An enormous range of fruiting trees and bushes, plus many other interesting and useful plants. The trust also runs training courses in agroforestry techniques.

46 Hunters Moon, Dartington, Totnes, Devon, TQ9 6JT

https://www.agroforestry.co.uk

Keepers Nursery

A great selection of over 600 varieties of fruit trees on different rootstocks, plus soft fruits, with an efficient delivery service.

Gallants Court, East Farleigh, Maidstone ME15 0LE

https://www.keepers-nursery.co.uk/

Walcott Organic Nursery Ltd

One of very few suppliers of organically grown fruit trees, with eighty varieties of apple and thirty varieties of plum, plus other fruit trees and soft fruits. A very helpful and friendly service.

Walcott Lane, Drakes Broughton, Pershore, Worcestershire, WR10 2AL

https://walcotnursery.co.uk

Useful Addresses

Societies and clubs

Amateur Entomologists' Society

A fun club for insect enthusiasts of all ages, with an annual insect fair at Kempton Park Racecourse, near London, where one can obtain all manner of books, equipment, live insects and more. The AES has a dedicated youth section with its own magazine.

https://www.amentsoc.org/

Bees, Wasps and Ants Recording Society (BWARS)

A society focused on *Hymenoptera*, with the particular aim of mapping the distributions of all of our bees, ants and wasps. This is vital work if we are to design sensible conservation strategies for the rare species. Members are encouraged to send in records of where they have seen particular species, which are then used to compile national maps. Biannual newsletter and maps free to members.

http://www.bwars.com/

Buglife

Focuses on conserving the UK's invertebrates (insects, spiders, slugs, snails, etc.). Buglife is actively involved in creating habitats for insects across the UK, and vocally campaigns against the worst pesticides.

https://www.buglife.org.uk/

Bumblebee Conservation Trust

A great little charity, involved in habitat creation for bumblebees and other pollinators. It also runs 'citizen science' schemes such as 'Beewalks', which is gathering valuable data on changing bumblebee populations.

https://www.bumblebeeconservation.org/

Butterfly Conservation

The oldest charity focused on insect conservation anywhere in the world, Butterfly Conservation does great work to look after both butterflies and moths.

https://butterfly-conservation.org/

Buzz Club

If you'd like to help scientists find out more about the pollinators that live in our gardens, to help us work out how best to help them, please consider joining the Buzz Club, a national organisation based at the University of Sussex. You can join in any of our range of fun garden experiments, learn a little about science, and find out more about what is living in your garden. You'll get an introductory pack with insect ID sheet, hand lens and wildflower seeds to grow. Some of the experiments are long-running, and we hope will continue indefinitely; others are one-off experiments to investigate specific questions, such as what types of organic materials make the best hoverfly lagoons, or which types of solitary bee hotel have the best uptake. Whichever ones you join in, you'll get a regular newsletter, feedback on your own results, and invitations to join any new experiments we launch.

www.thebuzzclub.uk

Royal Society for the Protection of Birds

Although primarily focused on birds, in recent years the RSPB has extended its remit to encompass all wildlife. A big and powerful organisation, it currently manages more than one hundred nature reserves around the UK.

https://www.rspb.org.uk/

Wildlife Trusts

Every county or region has its own wildlife trust. Between them, the wildlife trusts manage about 2,300 nature reserves, from remote woodlands to city nature parks. The wildlife trusts have an extensive volunteer network, and do much to help children engage with nature. Contact details for your local branch are readily obtained online.

Suppliers of equipment and books

NHBS (Natural History Book Service)

Sells the excellent Schwegler wood-concrete bumblebee nest box, plus an underground version of the same, in addition to a great range of equipment for ecological study, including butterfly nets, moth traps, cages for insect-rearing and much more. As the name suggests, it also stocks a huge range of natural history books.

https://www.nhbs.com

Nurturing Nature

Suppliers of excellent solitary bee boxes with viewing windows, carefully designed bumblebee nest boxes that work, wormeries and more.

www.nurturing-nature.co.uk

Watkins & Doncaster

Suppliers of a wonderful range of entomological equipment, books etc., including butterfly nets (ideal for close study and identification of bumblebees).

www.watdon.com

Soil testing for meadow-creation projects

For soil testing, you will need to first collect about 500 g of soil from your proposed meadow area. Using a trowel or spade, collect soil from just below the surface down to 15 cm, repeating at five sites scattered across the area, mixing the five samples to create a single, pooled sample. The sample should be sealed in a labelled plastic bag. A number of companies offer soil tests for samples sent through the post, including:

ELAB Ltd

About £15 per sample, but with a minimum charge of £60, so only viable if you wish to have several samples tested.

The Environmental Lab Ltd, Unit A2, Windmill Rd, St Leonards-on-Sea, East Sussex, TN38 9BY. 01424 718618 *sknight@elab-uk.co.uk* / *www.elab-uk.co.uk*

Eurofins

Approximately £17 per sample.

sales@eurofins.co.uk / *www.eurofinstesting.co.uk/samples/soil.html*

NRM laboratories

Coopers Bridge, Braziers Lane, Bracknell, Berkshire, RG42 6NS *enquiries@nrm.uk.com* / *www.nrm.uk.com*

Further Reading

If you would like to learn more about pollinators and wildlife gardening, try the books below:

Benton, T., *Bumblebees* (Harper Collins New Naturalist, 2006). An excellent and detailed account of all the British species, including their identification, and the most detailed account to date of their ecology.

Edwards, M. and Jenner, M., *A Field Guide to the Bumblebees of Great Britain & Ireland* (Ocelli, 2005). Very good-value identification guide based mainly on colour photographs and a simple colour chart.

Falk, S. and Lewington, R., *Field Guide to the Bees of Great Britain & Ireland* (Bloomsbury, 2015). A great guide to the UK's bees, beautifully illustrated.

Goulson, D., *Bumblebees; their behaviour, ecology and conservation* (Oxford University Press, 2010). A detailed review of the ecology of the world's bumblebees. Does not contain an identification guide.

———, *A Sting in the Tale* (Jonathan Cape, 2013). A *Sunday Times* bestseller about the lives of bumblebees.

———, *A Buzz in the Meadow* (Jonathan Cape, 2014). A popular science book about the wonderful lives of insects.

———, *The Garden Jungle* (Jonathan Cape, 2019). Describes the intricate network of fascinating small creatures living in our gardens and parks.

Else, G. R. and Edwards, M., *Handbook of the Bees of the British Isles* (Ray Society Monographs). An expensive two-volume tome, the definitive book on British bees for the very serious enthusiast.

Kirk, W. D. J. and Howes, F. N., *Plants for Bees: A guide to the plants that benefit the bees of the British Isles* (International Bee Research Association, Cardiff, 2012).

Prys-Jones, O. E. and Corbet, S. A., *Bumblebees* (Richmond Publishing Co., 1991). A really nice little book on UK bumblebees, with lovely paintings of all the British species, and good keys.

Stubbs, A. E. and Falk, S. J., *British Hoverflies* (British Entomological & Natural History Society, 2002). A great guide with lovely pictures.

Thompson, K., *The Book of Weeds* (Dorling Kindersley, 2009).

Thompson, K., *No Nettles Required: The Reassuring Truth about Wildlife Gardening* (Eden Project Books, 2007).

Thompson, K., *The Sceptical Gardener* (Icon, 2016).

Tolman, T. and Lewington, R., *Collins Butterfly Guide: The Most Complete Guide to the Butterflies of Britain and Europe* (Collins, 2009).

Walker, J., *Digging Deep in the Garden*, Books 1 and 2 (Earth-friendly, 2015 and 2016).

———, *How to Create an Ecogarden* (Aquamarine, 2011).

Waring, P., Townsend, M. and Lewington, R. *Field Guide to the Moths of Great Britain and Ireland*, Third Edition (Bloomsbury, 2018).